River Cafe Cook Book Two

Rose Gray and Ruth Rogers

Ebury Press London

Food Photography **Martyn Thompson**   Black and white Photography **Jean Pigozzi** Design **the Senate**

In the summer of 1994 the River Cafe was redesigned to create a larger, more exciting space, with an Italian wood-burning oven as its focus. Just as we were inspired by the char-grill ten years ago, we are now passionate about the oven's immediacy and responsiveness. It has opened up all kinds of opportunities for doing what we enjoy most – mixing the traditional with the modern.

We discovered how roasting at a high temperature intensifies the flavour of dishes such as porcini stuffed with pancetta and thyme. Roasting slowly, as the oven cools down, also has very special results – a shoulder of pork, for example, rubbed with fennel seeds, garlic and chilli achieves a succulent flavour reminiscent of 'porchetta', traditionally sold from vans and market stalls all over Tuscany. We wrap artichokes with thyme in foil, squash ripe plums and apricots on vanilla-scented bruschetta, stuff pheasants with ricotta and sage and cook them all in the wood oven.

Experimenting at home with our domestic ovens, we achieved the same delicious effects by roasting at a high temperature on the low rack of the oven. Equally, by slow roasting, and ideally using an oven brick to increase the moisture, you can roast overnight very successfully. All the recipes titled 'wood-roasted' use these techniques.

River Cafe Cook Book Two begins with seasonal fruit drinks as they begin the meals we serve in the restaurant. They range from freshly squeezed white peaches and sparkling dry Prosecco, an exuberant summer special, to freshly squeezed pomegranate mixed with campari and Prosecco, a delicious winter aperitivo with a beautiful colour.

Our second chapter, 'antipasti' in a traditional Italian meal, includes many of our favourite, simple starters – hardly recipes, just the pulling together of the finest ingredients to achieve classic dishes such as prosciutto with crisp Savoy cabbage, sweet aged balsamic vinegar and Parmesan, or a simple summer vegetarian carpaccio – slices of young zucchini marinated in lemon juice and extra virgin olive oil with shavings of Parmesan and herb rocket. These recipes and others reflect our open approach to planning a meal, with many dishes that can be eaten as part of a meal or work equally well on their own.

Fish has increasingly become a focus of our main courses, reflecting a change in our customers' preference. We have discovered and adapted many regional Italian recipes such as a variation on inzimino from Umbria, using salt cod, and baked whole loin of tuna with coriander from Sicily.

We have found new ways to cook duck, venison and game, changing traditional recipes to include other meats, for instance bollito misto with duck. Butchers have responded to our need to know about the breeds and feeds of animals and we love to cook the wonderful organic pork which is becoming increasingly available.

On recent trips to Italy we visited the wine and olive estates at Felsina and Selvapiana to select olive oil. We also went to the regions of Puglia and Sicily, where talking to cooks and producers we learned about their vegetables – cima di rape, ceci and cicoria – spices and the semolina bread called pagnotta.

The recipes in this, our second cookbook, have been stimulated by all these experiences and reflect the food we love to cook and eat at The River Cafe.

Rose Gray & **Ruth Rogers** London 1997

Dri

nks

1

Moscato d'asti con cedro fresco   Spumante con borra
Melone e prosecco   Fragole e prosecco   Lamponi
Pompelmo rosa e prosecco   Melagrana e prosecco

Bellini I   Bellini II   Arance sanguigne e prosecco
rosecco   Ribes nero e prosecco   More e prosecco

Moscato d'asti con cedro fresco
Moscato d'asti with fresh lime

For 6-8 This is a winter drink. You need to use a cocktail shaker with a perforated top.

6-8 limes, fridge cold
1 bottle Moscato d'Asti, cold

Squeeze the juice from 5 of the limes. Slice the sixth.

Pour the lime juice into the shaker. Add the Moscato very slowly, stirring gently, as it will immediately fizz up. Cover with the perforated top – this will stop the fizzing – and pour gently into champagne glasses. Serve with a slice of lime.

Spumante con borragine
Spumante secco with borage

For 6-8

150 g (5 oz) caster sugar
250 ml (8 fl oz) water
10-15 fresh borage leaves, washed
juice of 2 lemons
1 bottle Spumante Secco or Prosecco,
    fridge cold
at least 12-16 borage flowers

Using a small thick-bottomed saucepan, dissolve the sugar in the water, heating gently to make a syrup. When the syrup is hot, add the borage leaves. Stir and allow the borage to just wilt in the syrup. Remove from the heat, and cool. Strain the syrup, then add the lemon juice.

Put the syrup in a jug or cocktail shaker, add the wine (two-thirds wine to one-third syrup) and stir. Pour into champagne glasses, adding a few borage flowers to each glass.

Bellini I

For 6-8

8 ripe yellow peaches
100 g (4 oz) caster sugar
a good shot of Vecchio Romagna (Italian
    brandy)
1 bottle Prosecco, fridge cold

Preheat oven to 200° C/400° F/Gas 6.

Halve the peaches and remove the stones. Place the half peaches in a china baking dish and sprinkle with the caster sugar and Vecchio Romagna. Cover with foil and seal. Bake the peaches for 15-20 minutes. They should become slightly softer and the juices will begin to run. Remove from the oven and allow to cool.

Put the peaches and their juices in a food processor and pulse-chop. Push the pulp through a nylon fruit sieve.

Using a large cocktail shaker or jug with a lid, pour in 4 champagne glassfuls of peach purée, and add the same volume of Prosecco. Stir with a long spoon or stick to combine and also to prevent over-fizz. Pour into champagne glasses through the lid of the cocktail shaker.

Bellini II

For 6-8

10-12 ripe white peaches
1 bottle Prosecco, fridge cold

Choose very ripe white peaches. Cut them in half and remove the stones. Using an orange juicer, the rotary kind, press the juice from the peaches as you would from oranges.

Pour the peach juice into a jug or cocktail shaker with a lid. Add the same volume of Prosecco and stir to control the fizz and consequent overflow. Cover with the lid, and pour gently into champagne glasses.

Arance sanguigne e prosecco
Blood oranges and prosecco

For 6-8

8-9 blood oranges, according to juice
    obtained
1 bottle non-vintage Prosecco

Squeeze the oranges into a cocktail shaker or jug. Add a little Prosecco and stir with a spoon to still the fizz, then add about two-thirds of the remaining wine (you want to have slightly less orange juice than Prosecco). Pour into champagne glasses through the perforated top of the cocktail shaker.

Melone e prosecco
Melon and prosecco

For 6-8

1 very ripe cavaillon or canteloupe melon
juice of 1 lemon, or 1.1/2 limes
1 tablespoon caster sugar, or more
1 bottle Prosecco, fridge cold

Cut the melon in half. Scoop out the seeds and put them in a fruit sieve over a bowl to collect the juices. Scoop the rest of the ripe pulp from the skin and put in a food processor. Pulse-chop to liquefy. Sieve the pulp, adding it to the melon juices collected.

Add the lemon juice and 1 tablespoon sugar to the pulp. Add more or less sugar according to the sweetness of the melon.

Use a cocktail shaker or jug to mix the drink. Fill to slightly over half full with the melon juice. Add enough Prosecco to come to the top. Mix to combine and pour into champagne glasses through the perforated top of the shaker to contain excess fizz.

Fragole e prosecco
Strawberries and prosecco

For 6-8

500 g (18 oz) very ripe strawberries
juice of 1.1/2 lemons
2.1/2 tablespoons caster sugar
1 bottle Prosecco, fridge cold

Remove the hulls from the strawberries. If muddy, wash carefully, and lay out on a cloth to dry. Make sure the fruits are very dry.

Cut the strawberries in half and put in a food processor with the lemon juice and sugar. Pulse-chop to a liquid pulp. Strain the pulp through a fruit sieve.

Mix in a cocktail shaker equal parts of strawberry and Prosecco. Pour into champagne glasses using the perforated top of the shaker, as the drink will otherwise fizz up and over.

Lamponi e prosecco
Raspberries and prosecco

For 6-8

500 g (18 oz) ripe and sweet raspberries
100-150 g (4-5 oz) caster sugar
1 bottle Prosecco, fridge cold

Wash the raspberries and shake dry. Put in a food processor with the sugar, and pulse to a liquid. Push the pulp through a nylon fruit sieve.

Mix the pulp with the Prosecco in a large jug or cocktail shaker. Stir to calm the fizz and pour slowly into champagne glasses, using the lid to prevent overflow.

Ribes nero e prosecco
Blackcurrants and prosecco

For 6-8

250 g (9 oz) fresh blackcurrants, stalks
   removed
150 g (5 oz) caster sugar
1 bottle Prosecco, fridge cold

Wash the blackcurrants, and put in a saucepan with the sugar. Gently heat to allow the fruit to burst and release their juices. Do not boil. Remove from the heat and cool quickly. Push the pulp through a nylon fruit sieve.

Make sure the purée is completely cold, then mix with the Prosecco in a large jug or cocktail shaker. Stir to combine, then pour into champagne glasses. Use the lid to contain the fizz and prevent overflow as you pour.

More e prosecco
Blackberries and prosecco

For 6-8

3 punnets, about 400-500 g (14-18 oz), ripe
   blackberries
100 g (4 oz) caster sugar
1 bottle Prosecco, fridge cold

Put the blackberries and sugar in a food processor and pulse-chop to a purée. Push the purée through a nylon fruit sieve. Test for sweetness, as blackberries can be sour. Add more sugar if necessary.

Mix the purée in a jug or cocktail shaker with the cold Prosecco and pour into champagne glasses through the lid or top of the shaker to contain the fizz.

Pompelmo rosa e prosecco
Pink grapefruit and prosecco

For 6-8

3 pink grapefruit
200 ml (7 fl oz) Campari
1 bottle Prosecco, fridge cold

Squeeze the grapefruit and mix the juice with the Campari in a large jug or cocktail shaker. Stir to combine then slowly add the Prosecco. Pour into champagne glasses. Use the lid to prevent the fizz overflowing as you pour.

Melagrana e prosecco
Pomegranate and prosecco

For 6-8

10 pomegranates, very ripe
1 bottle Prosecco, fridge cold (or champagne)

Squeeze the juice from the halved pomegranates as you would oranges or lemons. Fill half a champagne glass with the juice, and top it up with Prosecco or champagne.

Salads
Mozzar
Frittata

ella

2

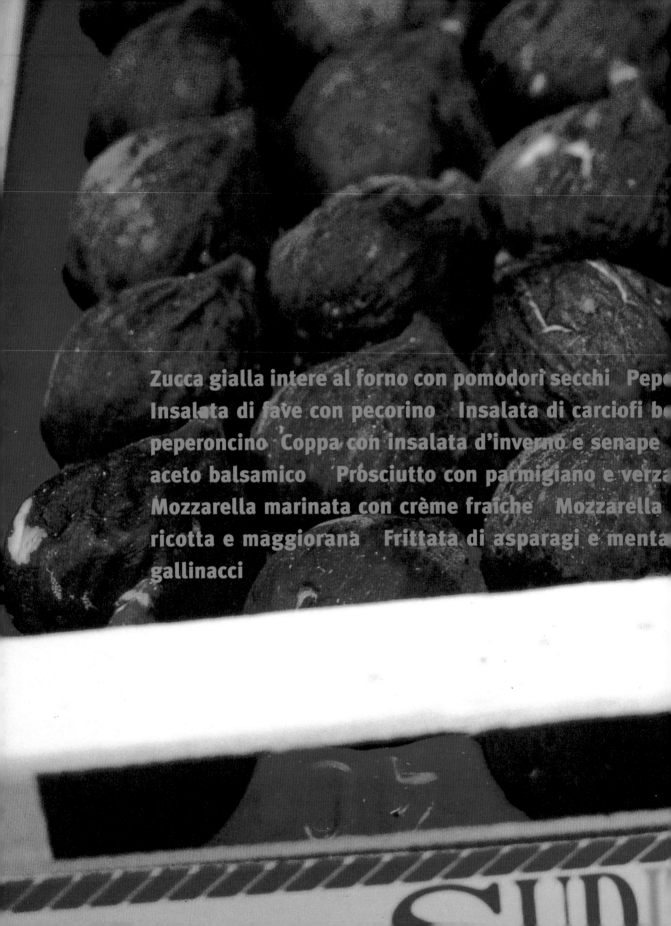

Zucca gialla intere al forno con pomodori secchi   Pep
Insalata di fave con pecorino   Insalata di carciofi b
peperoncino Coppa con insalata d'inverno e senape
aceto balsamico   Prosciutto con parmigiano e verza
Mozzarella marinata con crème fraîche   Mozzarella
ricotta e maggiorana   Frittata di asparagi e menta
gallinacci

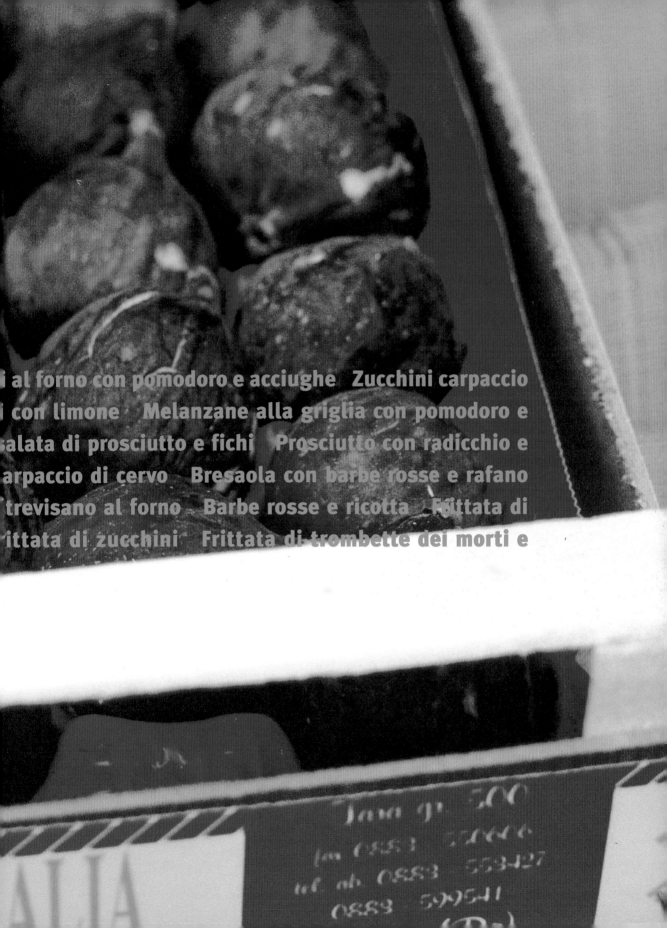

Zucca gialla intere al forno con pomodori secchi
Roasted squashes stuffed with sun-dried tomatoes

For 6 Use gem squashes for this recipe as they are portion-size.

6 whole gem squashes

12 sun-dried tomatoes, halved, or 100 g (4 oz) whole black olives, stoned

2 garlic cloves, peeled and cut into slivers

1 large bunch fresh thyme, leaves picked from the stalks

2 fresh red chillies, seeded and chopped

olive oil

Maldon salt and freshly ground black pepper

Preheat the oven to 200° C/400° F/Gas 6.

Trim the base of each squash so they stand firm. Cut a slice off the top large enough to allow you to scoop out the seeds.

Into each cavity put the sun-dried tomatoes or olives, 2 slivers of garlic, 1 small sprig of thyme, a little chopped chilli and a drizzle of olive oil. Season well with salt and pepper. Place the squashes into an oiled baking dish and cover with foil.

Bake in the preheated oven for 25 minutes. Remove the foil and continue cooking at a lower temperature of 150° C/300° F/Gas 2 until the flesh is soft, about another 10 minutes.

Peperoni al forno con pomodoro e acciughe
Baked peppers with tomatoes and anchovies

For 6

3 red and 3 yellow peppers
5 tablespoons olive oil
36 cherry tomatoes
3 garlic cloves, peeled and cut into slivers
24 salted anchovy fillets, prepared (see page 346)
1 bunch fresh basil or marjoram
100 g (4 oz) salted capers, prepared (see page 346)
Maldon salt and freshly ground black pepper

Preheat the oven to 180° C/350° F/Gas 4.

Halve each pepper lengthways and remove the core and seeds. Place the peppers in a lightly oiled baking dish, cut side up. Into each half pepper put 3 tomatoes, 2 slivers of garlic, 2 anchovy fillets, a few basil or marjoram leaves and 3-4 capers. Lightly drizzle the peppers with the remaining olive oil and season with salt and pepper.

Pour about 300 ml (10 fl oz) water into the base of the baking dish to prevent the peppers from sticking. Cover the dish tightly with foil. Bake in the preheated oven for 20 minutes, then remove from the oven. Remove the foil, and reduce the oven temperature to 120-150° C/250-300° F/Gas 1/2-2, and bake for a further 40 minutes or until the peppers are soft.

Zucchini carpaccio

For 6 Use only small young zucchini for this salad. Good varieties are Gold Rush, Tondo di Nizza and Bianco Friulano.

1 kg (2.1/4 lb) young yellow and green zucchini
225 g (8 oz) rocket
3 tablespoons extra virgin olive oil
juice of 1 lemon
Maldon salt and freshly ground black pepper
100-175 g (4-6 oz) Parmesan in the piece, sliced into slivers

Trim the ends off the zucchini and slice at an angle into thin rounds. Place in a bowl.

Pick through the rocket, discarding any yellow leaves. Snap off the stalks, then wash and dry the leaves thoroughly.

Mix together the olive oil, lemon juice and salt and pepper, and pour over the zucchini. Mix, then leave to marinate for 5 minutes. Season with salt and pepper.

Divide the rocket leaves between the serving plates. Put the zucchini on top, and then the Parmesan slivers. Add a small amount of freshly ground black pepper, and serve.

Insalata di fave con pecorino
Broad bean and pecorino salad

For 6

2.5 kg (5.1/2 lb) young broad beans in their pods
2 tablespoons aged balsamic vinegar
100 ml (3.1/2 fl oz) extra virgin olive oil
juice of 1 lemon
Maldon salt and freshly ground black pepper
1 bunch rocket, leaves picked from the stalks
1 bunch fresh mint, leaves picked from the stalks
150 g (5 oz) fresh Pecorino cheese, cut into thin slices
100 g (4 oz) Pecorino Staginata (aged), or Parmesan, shaved with a potato peeler

Pod the broad beans, and separate the larger lighter coloured beans from the smaller greener ones. Bring a large saucepan of water to the boil and blanch the larger beans for 3-5 minutes. Drain and peel off any tough skins.

Combine the raw and the cooked beans in a bowl and add the vinegar, oil and lemon juice. Toss together and season to taste with salt and pepper.

Combine the rocket and mint leaves in a large bowl, and gently mix in the dressed beans. Layer over this the pieces of both cheeses. Drizzle over a little extra balsamic vinegar and extra virgin olive oil. Serve immediately.

Insalata di carciofi bolliti con limone
Boiled lemon and artichoke heart salad

For 6

4 organic, thick-skinned lemons

6 small or 4 large artichokes with their stems

Maldon salt and freshly ground black pepper

150 g (5 oz) almonds, toasted

4 tablespoons soft raw honey

juice of 2 lemons

120 ml (4 fl oz) extra virgin olive oil

2 tablespoons fresh thyme leaves

Wash the lemons thoroughly, and put 3 of them whole into a small saucepan. Cover with water and add 100 g (4 oz) Maldon salt. Cover with the lid turned upside down so that the handle keeps the lemons below the surface of the water. Otherwise the lemons will float and not cook properly. Boil for 20 minutes. The lemons will become soft; the skin should easily be pierced with a fork. Drain and cool.

In boiling salted water, to which you have added the halved remaining lemon, cook the artichokes for 20 minutes or until one of the central leaves will come away with a little give. Drain and cool. Pull away the tough outside leaves, trim the stalks of string and fibre, and cut away the choke if there is any. Cut the hearts in halves, or quarters if they are large. Put in a salad bowl and season with salt and pepper.

Cut the boiled lemons in half and scoop out and discard the pulp and inner segments. Cut the soft skins into quarters and add to the artichoke hearts with the almonds.

Mix the honey with the lemon juice, then add the olive oil. Season and pour over the artichokes. Stir in the thyme.

Melanzane alla griglia con pomodoro e peperoncino
Grilled aubergines with tomato-chilli paste

For 6

3 large round, pale purple aubergines
extra virgin olive oil
5 garlic cloves, peeled and finely sliced
3 dried red chillies, crumbled
2 tablespoons dried wild oregano
2 x 800 g (1.3/4 lb) tins peeled plum tomatoes, drained of their juices (retain the
   juices)
Maldon salt and freshly ground black pepper
herb vinegar (Volpaia 'Erbe')
3 tablespoons fresh marjoram

Make the tomato-chilli paste first. Put 2 tablespoons oil in a thick-bottomed saucepan, and place over a medium heat. Add the garlic and gently cook until golden, then add the chilli and the oregano. Add the tomatoes and mash them into the garlic with a spoon. Stir and cook this pulp over a low heat for at least 45 minutes, stirring from time to time. The tomatoes should thicken and become almost dry. You may add a little of the drained juices if the tomatoes begin to stick. The colour should be an intense red and the texture sticky. Season with salt and black pepper and some olive oil. Spread over a flat plate and allow to dry out a bit.

Slice the aubergines 5 mm (1/4 in) thick and grill on a preheated very hot grill pan on both sides. Press to test and see whether they are cooked.

Arrange the slices on a serving plate, drizzle with herb vinegar and olive oil to taste, then spread with the tomato paste. Scatter with the marjoram leaves and serve.

Coppa con insalata d'inverno e senape
Coppa with winter leaves and mustard

For 6

24 very thin slices coppa di Parma
2 bunches rocket
2 heads red or white chicory
1 bunch dandelion leaves
2 heads trevise
Dressing
3 tablespoons balsamic vinegar
1.1/2 tablespoons Dijon mustard
extra virgin olive oil
Maldon salt and freshly ground black pepper

Trim all the salad leaves and place in a mixing bowl.

For the dressing, combine the balsamic vinegar and mustard. Thin with olive oil until it is a pourable consistency. Season with salt and pepper.

Toss the salad with half the dressing until each leaf is lightly coated. Divide between six plates in a small pile. Place the slices of coppa on the top and drizzle with the rest of the dressing.

Insalata di prosciutto e fichi
Prosciutto and fig salad

For 6 Ideally you should use purple basil and ripe black figs, or green basil and ripe green figs.

12 slices prosciutto crudo di San Daniele or Parma
9 ripe black or green figs
1 bunch fresh young mint
1 bunch fresh red or green basil
1 bunch rocket
juice of 1 lemon
4-6 tablespoons extra virgin olive oil
Maldon salt and freshly ground black pepper

Cut the figs in half.

Pick the young tender leaves from the mint, and select the smaller basil leaves. Pick over the rocket leaves, removing the larger stems. Wash and dry.

Mix the lemon juice with the olive oil, and season generously.

Toss the figs with the herb and rocket leaves and the dressing. Place on individual plates, combining the prosciutto slices into the salad as you do so.

Prosciutto con radicchio e aceto balsamico
Prosciutto and radicchio with balsamic vinegar

For 6

24 slices prosciutto
3 heads radicchio
300-400 g (10-14 oz) Parmesan in the piece
150 ml (5 fl oz) extra virgin olive oil
120 ml (4 fl oz) aged balsamic vinegar
1 tablespoon Dijon mustard
1/2-1 tablespoon Maldon salt
1 tablespoon freshly ground black pepper

Remove and discard the outer leaves from the radicchio. Cut each head in half, then, using a large, sharp and wide-bladed knife, shave into the finest possible shreds. Wash these shreds, then spin dry.

Using a potato peeler, or a small sharp knife, shave the Parmesan into slivers.

Mix the olive oil with the balsamic vinegar and mustard, and season to taste with the salt and pepper. Toss the radicchio shreds with the balsamic dressing.

Arrange the slices of prosciutto over each plate and cover with 2-3 tablespoons of the radicchio. Sprinkle with the Parmesan shavings. Drizzle a little extra virgin oil over each plate. Serve immediately.

Prosciutto con parmigiano e verza
Prosciutto, parmesan and savoy cabbage salad

For 6

24 slices prosciutto
1/2 fresh Savoy cabbage
175 ml (6 fl oz) extra virgin olive oil
Maldon salt and freshly ground black pepper
140 ml (4.1/2 fl oz) aged balsamic vinegar
300 g (10 oz) Parmesan in the piece

Use only the inner, paler leaves from the cabbage and, using a large, sharp and wide-bladed knife, shave the cabbage into the finest possible shreds. (You do not need to wash, as the inside of a Savoy is so tightly packed.) Place the shreds in a bowl, and add the olive oil and salt and pepper to taste. Toss together, then add the vinegar.

Break the Parmesan into little pieces using a pointed knife. Ease pieces away from the main piece so that they naturally separate along the crystals that form in the cheese. The pieces should be about 2-3 cm (1-1.1/4 in) long and up to 5 mm (1/4 in) thick. Add to the cabbage mixture and toss.

Arrange the slices of prosciutto over each plate and cover with 2 tablespoons of the cabbage and Parmesan mixture. You could dribble a little extra balsamic vinegar and extra virgin olive oil over each plate. Serve immediately.

Carpaccio di cervo
Venison carpaccio

For 6-8 Use the boned loins and fillets from the saddle of roe deer. The total weight of the two loins is usually around 650-700 g (a good 1.1/2 lb).

2 venison loin fillets (see above)
olive oil
Maldon salt and freshly ground black pepper
1 bunch fresh thyme, leaves picked from the stalks
juice of 2 lemons
1 bunch rocket leaves, washed

Preheat a char-grill or griddle pan.

Trim the venison loins of any fat and sinew. Brush all over with olive oil and generously season with pepper. Crush the thyme in a pestle and mortar with 2 tablespoons Maldon salt. Roll the loins in the crushed mixture. The oil will help the mixture to adhere to the meat.

Place the loins on the hot grill and turn and grill for a few minutes on each side. Do not burn the thyme, just allow the heat from the grill to seal the outside of the meat and form a crust. Allow the meat to cool.

Slice the cold loins as finely as you can. Then, using a very sharp wide-bladed carving knife, place the slices one at a time on a board. Press to flatten with the tip end of the blade, spreading the slice and enlarging it to double its original size.

Arrange the thin lacy slices to cover each plate. Season with salt and pepper, lemon juice and olive oil, and scatter over a few rocket leaves.

Bresaola con barbe rosse e rafano
Bresaola, beetroot and horseradish salad

For 6

12 small young red beetroots
6 golden beetroots
5 cm (2 in) stick fresh horseradish
36 thin slices bresaola (6 per person)
5 tablespoons fresh tarragon, leaves picked from the stalks, or herb rocket leaves
120 ml (4 fl oz) extra virgin olive oil
juice of 2 lemons
Maldon salt and freshly ground black pepper

Trim the beetroot leaves 3 cm (1.1/4 in) from the bulbs, and gently wash both leaves and bulbs. (Keep the leaves for another dish, see page 60.) Put the bulbs in a saucepan and cover with cold water. Bring to the boil, and simmer for 30 minutes. Test for doneness by pressing a beet between your fingers. Remove the skin – it rubs off very easily. Cut each beetroot into eighths.

Peel, then grate the horseradish. Use a medium grater which makes mini slivers.

Arrange the bresaola slices over each plate. Divide the beetroot between the plates over the bresaola. Scatter over the tarragon or rocket, then the horseradish. Mix together the oil, lemon juice and salt and pepper, and pour this dressing over the salad.

Mozzarella marinata con crème fraîche
Marinated mozzarella and crème fraîche

For 6 This is our version of burrata, a southern Italian dish which can be bought in good cheese shops – sliced fresh buffalo mozzarella, marinated in fresh cream.

6 buffalo mozzarella, about 120 g (4.1/2 oz) each
Maldon salt and freshly ground black pepper
extra virgin olive oil
2 tablespoons each of roughly chopped fresh basil, marjoram, mint and oregano
300 g (10 oz) crème fraîche
1 bunch rocket, trimmed
juice of 1 lemon
6 thick slices pugliese or sourdough bruschetta (see page 290)
extra virgin olive oil

Cut the mozzarella into 8 mm (1/3 in) slices into a large flat dish, then season with salt and pepper. Pour over 100 ml (3.1/2 fl oz) of the olive oil and sprinkle over half the fresh chopped herbs. Spoon over the crème fraîche, then turn the cheese slices in this to coat and cover. Sprinkle the remaining herbs on top.

Serve the marinated mozzarella with the bruschetta and the rocket leaves tossed with the lemon juice and some extra virgin olive oil.

Mozzarella con trevisano al forno
Baked mozzarella with trevise

For 6

6 buffalo mozzarella, each approx. 120 g (4.1/2 oz) in weight and sliced into 3

4 heads trevise

1 bunch fresh marjoram

2 dried red chillies, crumbled

Maldon salt and freshly ground black pepper

3 tablespoons Volpaia 'Erbe' vinegar or balsamic vinegar

olive oil

100 g (4 oz) Parmesan, freshly grated

100 g (4 oz) pine nuts, lightly toasted

6 thick slices pugliese or sourdough bruschetta (see page 290)

Preheat the oven to 200° C/400° F/Gas 6.

Depending on the size of the trevise heads, cut them into quarters or eighths lengthways; the stem should remain attached to the leaves. Lay the trevise pieces in a baking tray, and sprinkle with fresh marjoram, chilli, salt, pepper and vinegar, and drizzle with oil. Bake in the preheated oven for 5 minutes.

Place the mozzarella slices over the top of the baked trevise, then sprinkle with the Parmesan. Place back in the very hot oven until the mozzarella has melted, a few minutes only.

Serve the bruschetta with the trevise and mozzarella. Sprinkle the toasted pine nuts over the dish as you serve.

Barbe rosse e ricotta
Beetroot, ricotta and beet leaf salad

For 6

1 recipe Wood-roasted whole beetroots (see page 156)
the leaves of the beetroots
Maldon salt and freshly ground black pepper
100 ml (3.1/2 fl oz) extra virgin olive oil
2.1/2 tablespoons herb vinegar (Volpaia 'Erbe')
3 fresh red chillies, seeded and finely chopped
1 bunch rocket leaves, washed and dried
500 g (18 oz) fresh ricotta in the piece, cut into 6 thin slices
1 small bunch fresh marjoram, leaves picked from the stalks

Sort out the tender leaves from the beetroots and remove the stalks. Wash carefully and blanch for 2 minutes in boiling salted water. Spread out to drain and cool.

To make the chilli sauce, mix together 3 tablespoons of the olive oil and the chilli.

Mix together the remaining oil and the vinegar, and season. Cut each beetroot into halves and halves again. Toss with a few tablespoons of this chilli-free dressing.

Divide the rocket leaves between the plates. Toss the blanched beetroot leaves in the remaining chilli-free dressing, and mix with the rocket. Place the quartered beetroots amongst the beet and rocket leaves, and cover with the slices of ricotta.

Sprinkle with the marjoram and spoon over a little of the chilli sauce.

Frittata di ricotta e maggiorana
Ricotta and marjoram frittata

For 6

8 organic eggs
100 g (4 oz) fresh ricotta cheese, lightly beaten with a fork
2 tablespoons chopped fresh marjoram
50 g (2 oz) Parmesan, freshly grated
Maldon salt and freshly ground black pepper
2 tablespoons olive oil

Preheat the oven to 200° C/400° F/Gas 6.

Break the eggs into a bowl and beat lightly. Add 75 g (3 oz) of the ricotta, reserving the rest, together with most of the marjoram, most of the Parmesan, and salt and pepper to taste. Stir to combine.

In a small 20-25 cm (8-10 in) ovenproof frying pan, heat the olive oil, tilting the pan to coat all sides. Add the egg mixture and lower the heat. Cook over a low heat, loosening the eggs at the sides from time to time, until just set – it should be quite runny.

Scatter with the rest of the marjoram and ricotta, and place in the hot oven for a few seconds only. Loosen the frittata from the pan with a long spatula and put on to a warm plate. Scatter over the remaining Parmesan and cut into wedges to serve.

Frittata di asparagi e menta
Asparagus and mint frittata

For 6

8 organic eggs
225 g (8 oz) sprue asparagus
Maldon salt and freshly ground black pepper
50 g (2 oz) Parmesan, freshly grated
1 small bunch fresh mint, leaves picked from the stalks, finely chopped
2 tablespoons olive oil

Preheat the oven to 200° C/400° F/Gas 6.

Cut off and discard the tough ends of the asparagus, and blanch the spears in boiling water until just tender. Drain, dry, then season with salt and pepper.

Break the eggs into a bowl and beat lightly. Add most of the Parmesan and mint, reserving a little for the end. Season with salt and pepper to taste.

Cook the frittata in the ovenproof frying pan as opposite. Just before placing it in the hot oven, put the asparagus and the remaining Parmesan and mint on top. Serve as opposite.

Frittata di zucchini
Zucchini frittata

For 6

8 organic eggs
4 small or 3 medium zucchini
3 tablespoons olive oil
2 garlic cloves, peeled and chopped
1 small bunch fresh basil, leaves picked from the stalks and roughly chopped
Maldon salt and freshly ground black pepper
50 g (2 oz) Parmesan, grated

Preheat the oven to 200° C/400° F/Gas 6.

Trim the zucchini, then cut thinly at an angle. Heat 2 tablespoons of the oil in an ovenproof frying pan. Add the garlic followed by the zucchini slices. When brown on all sides, add most of the basil and salt and pepper to taste. The zucchini should be quite dry; if there is any oil remaining, drain through a sieve and reserve.

Break the eggs into a bowl and beat lightly. Add the zucchini and garlic, reserving 1 tablespoon for the end. Season with salt and pepper.

Cook the frittata in the ovenproof frying pan as on page 44, using the reserved oil as well as the further tablespoon if necessary. Just before placing it into the hot oven, spread the rest of the zucchini on top. Remove from the oven and sprinkle with the Parmesan and the remaining basil. Serve as on page 44.

Frittata di trombette dei morti e gallinacci
Trompettes de mort and girolles frittata

For 6

8 organic eggs
350 g (12 oz) trompettes de mort
225 g (8 oz) chanterelles
3 tablespoons olive oil
2 garlic cloves, peeled and thinly sliced
a handful of chopped fresh basil or parsley
Maldon salt and freshly ground black pepper
25 g (1 oz) Parmesan, grated

Cut off the stalk end of the trompettes. Wash the trompettes by plunging them briefly into cold water and dry in a salad spinner. Cut off the stalk ends of the chanterelles. Clean with a brush.

Heat 2 tablespoons of the olive oil in a pan and add the garlic. Cook quickly until tender, then remove from the pan and drain. Retain the oil and return it to the pan. Add the chanterelles and fry for a minute or two, then add the trompettes and cook for a further few minutes. Add the basil or parsley, and salt and pepper to taste.

Break the eggs into a bowl and beat lightly. Add three-quarters of the mushroom mixture, and season with salt and pepper.

Cook the frittata in the ovenproof frying pan as on page 44, using the reserved oil as well as the further tablespoon if necessary. Just before placing it in the hot oven, put the rest of the mushrooms on top, along with the Parmesan. Serve as on page 44.

Past

Pole

a

nta

3

Pasta all'uovo   Pasta verde   Ravioli di patate e rucol
Rotolo verde con ricotta e erbe d'estiva   Tagliatelle c
Pappardelle con cavolo nero e lenticchie   Zucchini ca
bianchi   Spaghetti con rucola e ricotta   Linguini con
con cozze delle marche   Spaghetti alle vongole   S
Penne con zucchini e ricotta   Bucatini con acciughe
Polenta con tartufi bianchi   Polenta con porcini fresc

avioli ripiene di bietole   Ravioli di zucca e mascarpone
ascarpone e pangrattato   Tagliatelle con salsa di noci
ara   Tagliatelle con gallinacci   Tagliatelle con tartufi
fresche   Spaghetti con aragosta marinata   Spaghetti
ettini con calamari   Penne con broccoli e olive verdi
angrattato   Polenta in brodo di pollo con cavolo nero

Pasta all'uovo
Fresh pasta

Makes about 1 kg (2.1/4 lb) This is made in a food processor or mixer fitted with a dough hook. It is important to use Italian pasta flour labelled Tipo 'OO' (a soft wheat finely ground pasta flour).

700 g (a good 1.1/2 lb) Tipo 'OO' flour
4 medium fresh organic eggs
9 medium egg yolks, from fresh organic eggs
1 tablespoon Maldon salt
1 tablespoon olive oil
semolina flour for dusting

Sieve the flour into the bowl of a food processor or mixer. Add the eggs, egg yolks, salt and olive oil to the centre. Using a dough hook, knead slowly, allowing the mixture to come together. Keep on a low speed for 10 minutes. The ball of dough should become smooth. If it is too dry to hold together, add another egg.

Dust your work surface with semolina flour. Divide the dough in half, and knead each half by hand for 3-4 minutes until completely smooth. Wrap each ball of dough in cling film and put in the fridge to chill for 1.1/2-2 hours.

To prepare your dough for cutting into either tagliatelle or ravioli, put it through a pasta machine. Put each ball through at the thickest setting ten times, folding the sheet into three each time to get a short thick strip, and then turn it by a quarter, and put it through the machine again. After ten such folds the pasta feels silky. Only then reduce the setting gradually down to the thinness required.

If rolling by hand, hand-knead and hand-roll the dough the equivalent of ten times through the machine. Do this in a cool place so the pasta does not become dry.

Pasta verde
Spinach pasta

Makes about 1 kg (2.1/4 lb)

700 g (a good 1.1/2 lb) pasta flour
2 medium fresh organic eggs
9 medium egg yolks, from fresh organic eggs
2 egg-sized balls of blanched spinach, squeezed dry and finely chopped
1 tablespoon Maldon salt
semolina flour for dusting

In your processor or mixer fitted with a dough hook, combine the flour with the eggs and egg yolks, then add the spinach and salt. Keeping on a low speed, knead the dough as for Fresh Pasta. If the dough seems too sticky, add a little extra flour. The dough should become silky after about 10 minutes.

Remove on to a floured surface, and cut into two. Knead each ball of dough separately by hand for 3-4 minutes. Wrap in cling film and put in the fridge to chill for 1.1/2-2 hours.

Prepare the spinach dough as for Fresh Pasta.

Ravioli di patate e rucola
Ravioli with potato and rocket

For 8 Use Pecorino Romano, a salty cheese with the same crystalline formation as Parmesan.

1 recipe Fresh Pasta (see page 54)

semolina flour for dusting

100 ml (3.1/2 fl oz) extra virgin olive oil

50 g (2 oz) aged farmhouse Pecorino Romano cheese, grated

200 g (7 oz) rocket, washed, dried and roughly chopped

Filling

2 kg (4.1/2 lb) red-skinned Desirée potatoes, scrubbed clean (do not peel)

Maldon salt and freshly ground black pepper

3-4 tablespoons extra virgin olive oil

4 garlic cloves, peeled and finely chopped

2-3 small dried red chillies, crumbled

1.15 kg (2 lb, 9 oz) rocket, washed and dried

100 g (4 oz) aged farmhouse Pecorino Romano cheese, grated

Boil the potatoes in salted water until soft. Cool. Scrape off and discard the skin, and put the flesh through a coarse mouli.

Heat the oil in a large heavy thick-bottomed pan and fry the garlic and chilli until the garlic is just turning gold. Add 800 g (1.3/4 lb) of the rocket, stir briefly, then put on the lid and immediately remove from the heat. This allows the rocket to wilt in the steam generated. Cool, then drain off excess liquid and chop the rocket finely.

Roughly chop the remaining raw rocket for the filling.

In a large cold mixing bowl mix together the mashed potato, the chopped wilted rocket, the chopped raw rocket, and the Pecorino. Season with black pepper and salt to taste (but be sparing with the latter as the Pecorino is salty).

Divide the pasta into balls the size of a large egg. Using a pasta machine, roll them out into long strips (one at a time to prevent drying) as thin as possible. Cut in half if too long.

Put tablespoons of filling about 6 cm (2.1/4 in) apart on the sheet, in the centre of the half nearest you, so that you can fold the other half over to make a 'parcel' of about 5 cm (2 in) square. Brush around the fillings with a pastry brush dipped in water before folding, so that the envelopes you are making will seal properly. Using a pasta cutter, seal each envelope by cutting on three sides (the fourth is the fold). Dust a large plate or tray with semolina flour and carefully place the ravioli on it, making sure that they do not touch. You should have about fifty.

Bring a large pan of salted water to the boil, and put in the ravioli. Lower heat to a simmer: the ravioli will rise to the surface of the water after 30 seconds, but according to how thin you managed to roll the pasta, they will take from 3-5 minutes to cook. Test on the join where the pasta is thickest; it should be al dente.

Serve the ravioli with a drizzle of extra virgin olive oil, grated Pecorino and a scattering of chopped fresh rocket.

Ravioli ripiene di bietole
Ravioli with beet leaves

For 8

1 recipe Fresh Pasta (see page 54)

semolina flour for dusting

Sage Butter (see opposite)

Filling

500 g (18 oz) tender leaves from young beetroots, stalks removed

Maldon salt and freshly ground black pepper

1 small red onion, peeled and finely chopped

100 g (4 oz) unsalted butter

4 tablespoons fresh marjoram leaves

1 garlic clove, peeled and finely chopped

150 g (5 oz) ricotta cheese, lightly broken up with a fork

100 g (4 oz) Parmesan, grated

1/2 nutmeg, freshly grated

Wash the beetroot leaves and blanch in salted water for 4 minutes. Drain and lay out on a tray to dry. Chop finely.

Gently fry the onion in the butter in a large heavy-bottomed pan until the onion begins to brown. Add the marjoram and garlic, stir for 1 minute, then add the beet leaves. Just cook together briefly, season and allow to cool.

Stir the beet leaves and Parmesan into the ricotta. Add nutmeg and season.

Make the ravioli as described in the previous recipe. Serve with Sage Butter.

Ravioli di zucca e mascarpone
Ravioli with pumpkin and mascarpone

For 8

1 recipe Fresh Pasta (see page 54)
semolina flour for dusting
Filling
about 1.5 kg (3.1/4 lb) pumpkin or squash, cooked (see page 158)
50 g (2 oz) unsalted butter
2 large garlic cloves, peeled and finely sliced
1 bunch fresh marjoram, leaves picked from the stalks
Maldon salt and freshly ground black pepper
500 g (18 oz) mascarpone cheese
500 g (18 oz) Parmesan, freshly grated
1/2 nutmeg, freshly grated
Sage butter
2 bunches fresh sage, leaves picked from the stalks
200 g (7 oz) unsalted butter, clarified

Cool the cooked pumpkin or squash, discard the skin and mash the flesh. In a heavy-bottomed saucepan, melt the butter and cook the garlic until golden. Add the marjoram and the mashed pumpkin, combine and taste for seasoning. When cool, stir in the mascarpone, Parmesan and nutmeg.

Make the ravioli as in the potato ravioli recipe. For the sage butter, heat the clarified butter in a small pan and, when hot, add the sage leaves for a second or two. Remove from the heat.

Cook the ravioli as in the potato ravioli recipe, then serve with the sage butter.

Rotolo verde con ricotta e erbe d'estiva
Spinach pasta with ricotta and summer herbs

For 6

1 recipe Spinach Pasta (see page 55)

Maldon salt and freshly ground black pepper

semolina flour for dusting

Parmesan, freshly grated

Olive paste

250 g (9 oz) stoned black Niçoise olives

2 garlic cloves, peeled

3 tablespoons fresh basil

3 tablespoons fresh marjoram

Filling

750 g (1 lb, 10 oz) ricotta cheese

150 g (5 oz) Parmesan, freshly grated

4 tablespoons chopped fresh basil

3 tablespoons chopped fresh marjoram

3 tablespoons chopped fresh parsley

3 organic eggs

120 ml (4 fl oz) double cream

Nutmeg butter

225 g (8 oz) unsalted butter, clarified

1 nutmeg

To make the olive paste, put the olives, garlic, basil and marjoram into the bowl of a food processor and pulse-chop. Remove to a bowl and set aside.

To make the filling, beat the ricotta with a fork to lighten and separate it. Add the Parmesan, the basil, marjoram and parsley, and season with salt and pepper to taste. Take about half of this herb ricotta, and place in the (cleaned) bowl of the food processor. Pulse-chop to combine and then add the eggs one by one. Finally add the cream and mix in. You will have a bright green, fairly liquid mixture. Carefully fold this mixture into the remaining ricotta mix to combine, and then season to taste.

Roll the pasta out by hand on a work surface, dusted with semolina flour, to a large sheet, as thin as possible; it will not matter if there are a few holes or tears. Cut the edges to straighten; you should have a piece of about 30 cm (12 in) square.

If you have a pasta machine, roll out two strips and join to make the same size by brushing the edges with water to seal.

Spread the olive paste along the edge of the side nearest you, and then spread the ricotta mixture over the rest of the sheet to a 1 cm (1/2 in) thickness. Scatter with a little grated Parmesan. Starting with the olive edge, gently roll the pasta up into a large sausage, about 6 cm (2.1/2 in) thick. Wrap the roll in a large tea towel as tightly as you can, securing with string to help keep the roll in shape. (If you do not have a fish kettle, the best cooking pot for this long roll, you will have to cut the roll in half and make two tea-towel wrapped parcels.)

Fill the fish kettle or other suitable pan with water and bring to the boil. Add salt generously and poach the pasta roll for about 20-25 minutes.

Meanwhile, make the nutmeg butter. After clarifying the butter, grate the whole nutmeg into it, and season with salt and pepper. Heat gently.

Drain the pasta roll and remove from the cloth. Place on a board and cut into generous 2 cm (3/4 in) slices. Ladle the nutmeg butter over, and sprinkle with some grated Parmesan.

Tagliatelle con mascarpone e pangrattato

For 6 as a starter

600 g (1 lb, 6 oz) fresh tagliatelle or 450 g (1 lb) dried egg tagliatelle

500 g (18 oz) mascarpone cheese

4 organic egg yolks

200 ml (7 fl oz) extra virgin olive oil

4 garlic cloves, peeled and finely chopped

150 g (5 oz) Parmesan, freshly grated

Maldon salt and freshly ground black pepper

Herb pangrattato

1 ciabatta loaf, bottom crust removed, made into coarse crumbs

200 ml (7 fl oz) extra virgin olive oil

6 garlic cloves, peeled and left whole

3 tablespoons each of chopped fresh thyme and marjoram

Slowly mix the mascarpone and egg yolks together in a food processor. Add the oil, drop by drop, as for mayonnaise. Stir in the chopped garlic and Parmesan. Season.

Heat the oil for the pangrattato in a small saucepan and add the whole garlic cloves. Cook gently until a deep golden colour, then remove the cloves. Add the breadcrumbs to the garlic-flavoured oil and cook until golden. Just before they turn brown, add the herbs. Immediately remove the breadcrumbs and herbs from the oil using a slotted spoon, and drain on kitchen paper.

Cook the tagliatelle in a large pan of boiling salted water until al dente, then drain. Mix with the mascarpone and generously cover with the herb pangrattato.

Tagliatelle con salsa di noci
Tagliatelle with walnut sauce

For 6 as a starter

600 g (1 lb, 6 oz) fresh tagliatelle or 450 g (1 lb) dried egg tagliatelle

2 kg (4.1/2 lb) wet walnuts, shelled and bitter skins removed

breadcrumbs from 1 loaf ciabatta bread, stale if possible, soaked in 150 ml (5 fl oz)
   milk

3 garlic cloves, peeled

Maldon salt and freshly ground black pepper

2 tablespoons roughly chopped fresh flat-leaf parsley

150 ml (5 fl oz) olive oil

100 g (4 oz) Parmesan, freshly grated

4 tablespoons roughly chopped fresh basil

75 g (3 oz) soft unsalted butter

Keeping a few pieces of walnut whole for serving, pound the remainder together with the garlic in a mortar. Add a little salt and then the parsley, and continue to pound.

Squeeze most of the milk from the breadcrumbs (keep the milk). Add half of the breadcrumbs to the mortar, and mix in. Add the olive oil gradually, plus a little of the milk to loosen the paste, stirring continuously; the sauce must be well amalgamated. Finally, add half the Parmesan and basil, then season. The result is a thick green sauce.

Cook the tagliatelle in a generous amount of boiling salted water, then drain thoroughly and return to the saucepan. Add the softened butter and stir in the sauce.

Serve with the rest of the basil, Parmesan and a few pieces of uncrushed walnut.

Pappardelle con cavolo nero e lenticchie
Pappardelle with cavolo nero and lentils

For 6 as a starter

3 heads cavolo nero, stalks removed, blanched and roughly chopped

2 tablespoons olive oil

150 g (5 oz) pancetta, cut into matchsticks

1 small red onion, peeled and finely sliced

1/2 head celery, stalks and leaves chopped

1 teaspoon chopped fresh rosemary leaves

1 garlic clove, peeled

120 ml (4 fl oz) Chianti Classico wine

150 ml (5 fl oz) Chicken Stock (see page 142)

Maldon salt and freshly ground black pepper

200 g (7 oz) Castelluccio or Puy lentils, cooked (see page 347)

600 g (1 lb, 6 oz) fresh pappardelle or 450 g (1 lb) dried

100 g (4 oz) Parmesan, freshly grated

extra virgin olive oil

Heat the oil in a heavy-bottomed pan and fry the pancetta slowly to release the fat, then add the onion and celery stalks. Cook until they begin to colour, then add the rosemary and garlic, and fry for 5 minutes. Add the wine and cook briefly until reduced.

Heat the stock. Add the lentils to the pancetta mixture, stir and cook to combine for 3-4 minutes. Add the cavolo and enough stock to liquefy the mixture. Heat through.

Cook the pappardelle then drain well. Mix into the lentil mixture, then add the Parmesan. Toss and serve with oil drizzled over and sprinkled with the celery leaves.

Zucchini carbonara
Tagliatelle with deep-fried zucchini

For 6 as a starter

900 g (2 lb) small young fresh zucchini, trimmed

250 ml (8 fl oz) olive oil

600 g (1 lb, 6 oz) fresh tagliatelle or 450 g (1 lb) dried egg tagliatelle

Maldon salt and freshly ground black pepper

1 small dried red chilli, crumbled

5 medium organic eggs, lightly beaten

200 g (7 oz) Pecorino cheese (Staginata), grated

1 bunch fresh basil, cut into ribbons

Cut the zucchini into fine dice. Heat the olive oil in a thick-bottomed pan, and when hot fry the diced zucchini in batches, one layer at a time. They take seconds to brown on the edges and become crisp. Remove and drain on kitchen paper.

Cook the pasta in a generous amount of boiling salted water, then drain thoroughly. Season with salt and pepper and the crumbled dried chilli, and return to the hot saucepan. Add the beaten eggs and stir to combine, allowing the egg to cook just by contact with the hot pasta. Add the zucchini dice, half the Pecorino and the basil. Serve with the remaining grated Pecorino on top.

Tagliatelle con gallinacci
Tagliatelle with girolles

For 6 as a starter

600 g (1 lb, 6 oz) fresh tagliatelle (see page 54) or 450 g (1 lb) dried tagliatelle

1 kg (2.1/4 lb) fresh girolles

3 tablespoons olive oil

4 garlic cloves, peeled and finely chopped

juice of 1 lemon

Maldon salt and freshly ground black pepper

1 bunch fresh flat-leaf parsley, leaves picked from the stalks, finely chopped

150 g (5 oz) unsalted butter, softened

150 g (5 oz) Parmesan, grated

Pick through the girolles, brushing out any leaves or moss, or bits of earth or sand. Trim the stalks. Tear them in halves, quarters or eighths lengthways, according to size, so that the stalks remain attached to the cups. You are aiming to echo the width of the tagliatelle with the pieces of girolle.

Heat the olive oil in a pan until smoking, then add the girolles and toss. Add the garlic and cook over a high heat for a minute or two. Add the lemon juice, and season with salt, pepper and parsley.

Cook the tagliatelle in a generous amount of boiling salted water until al dente, then drain. Add the butter, girolles and Parmesan to the tagliatelle and serve with extra Parmesan.

Tagliatelle con tartufi bianchi
Tagliatelle with white truffles

For 6 as a starter

600 g (1 lb, 6 oz) fresh tagliatelle (or tagliarini) or 450 g (1 lb) dried egg tagliatelle (or
 tagliarini)
white truffles, 30 g (1.1/4 oz) per person
Maldon salt and freshly ground black pepper
200 g (7 oz) unsalted butter, softened
3 tablespoons grated Parmesan

Clean the truffles with a soft brush to remove all sand and grit. If there is any clay clinging, use a small pointed knife to scrape it off. Never use water.

Cook the pasta in a generous amount of boiling salted water, then drain thoroughly, saving a little of the water. Stir in three-quarters of the softened butter and a few tablespoons of the pasta water. Season with salt and pepper, add the Parmesan, and toss together.

Grate the first few shavings from each truffle into the pasta, and toss. Serve on warm plates, and place a little knob of the softened remaining butter on top. Generously shave the truffles all over each portion. Serve with extra Parmesan.

Spaghetti con rucola e ricotta
Spaghetti with rocket and ricotta

For 6 as a starter

1 kg (2.1/4 lb) rocket leaves

100 ml (3.1/2 fl oz) extra virgin olive oil

3 garlic cloves, peeled and roughly chopped

4 tablespoons fresh basil leaves, torn into pieces

2 fresh red chillies, seeded and chopped

Maldon salt and freshly ground black pepper

400 g (14 oz) spaghetti

200 g (7 oz) ricotta, lightly beaten with a fork

150 g (5 oz) Parmesan, grated

Wash the rocket and dry in a salad spinner. Divide the quantity in half, and roughly chop one of these halves.

Heat a large saucepan and add 2 tablespoons of the oil. Gently fry the garlic until it begins to turn gold, then add the torn-up basil leaves and the whole rocket leaves. Put on the lid and let the rocket wilt – this takes 2-3 minutes. Put the hot wilted rocket and any liquid in the pan in a food processor and pulse-chop. Add half of the chopped rocket and blend again to combine. Stir in the chilli, salt, pepper and the remaining olive oil.

Cook the spaghetti in plenty of boiling salted water. Drain, return to the pan, and add the rocket sauce. Turn the pasta over gently to coat each strand. Finally, lightly fork in the ricotta and the remaining chopped rocket. Season, and serve with the Parmesan.

Linguini con fave fresche
Linguini with fresh broad beans

For 6 as a starter Make this pasta only when broad beans are young and tender.

400 g (14 oz) podded broad beans

1 small red onion, peeled and finely chopped

2 garlic cloves, peeled and finely chopped

1 small bunch fresh parsley, chopped

4 tablespoons olive oil

250 ml (8 fl oz) hot water

400 g (14 oz) linguini

Maldon salt and freshly ground black pepper

100 g (4 oz) Parmesan, freshly grated

In a large heavy saucepan cook the onion, garlic and parsley slowly in the oil for 5 minutes or until very soft. Add the broad beans and stir for several minutes. Add the water and cook until the beans are tender. Add salt and pepper. Put half of the beans in the food processor and pulse-chop to a coarse purée. Return to and mix with the whole beans.

Cook the linguini in plenty of boiling salted water until al dente. Drain, then add to the sauce and stir. Check for seasoning and serve with the Parmesan.

Spaghetti con aragosta marinata
Marinated lobster spaghetti

For 6 We use 'crippled' lobsters, which are usually much cheaper. You have to order them in advance from your fishmonger. Serve this pasta as a main course.

6 x 450 g (1 lb) lobsters, or 3 large or 3-4 medium lobsters

Maldon salt and freshly ground black pepper

1 branch bay leaves

1 large fresh red chilli

1 head garlic

600 g (1 lb, 6 oz) spaghetti

1 bunch flat-leaf parsley, leaves picked from the stalks, chopped

3 lemons, halved

Marinade

2 garlic cloves, peeled

juice of 3 lemons

120 ml (4 fl oz) extra virgin olive oil

1 small dried red chilli, crumbled

Put the lobsters in a very large saucepan of cold salted water. They should be completely covered. Use two saucepans if necessary. Add the bay, fresh chilli and garlic to the water, and place the pan over a low heat. Bring to the boil very slowly. The lobsters will remain asleep and die without suffering.

When the water has come to the boil, take the lobsters out and allow to cool. Remove all the meat from the shells, dividing the bodies into two or three large pieces each.

For the marinade, crush the garlic with a teaspoon of sea salt, and add to the lemon juice and olive oil. Season with salt and pepper and the dried chilli. Marinate the lobster pieces for 30 minutes.

Cook the spaghetti in a generous amount of boiling salted water, then drain and return to the pan. Add the lobster and marinade. Heat through, stir in the parsley, season and serve with lemon halves.

Spaghetti con cozze delle marche
Spaghetti with mussels

For 6 as a starter

3 kg (6.1/2 lb) mussels, cleaned

4 tablespoons olive oil

3 garlic cloves, peeled and chopped

1 small dried red chilli, crumbled

2 tablespoons chopped fresh oregano

150 ml (5 fl oz) white wine (Verdicchio Classico)

1 kg (2.1/4 lb) ripe tomatoes, skinned, seeded and chopped

Maldon salt and freshly ground black pepper

3 tablespoons chopped fresh flat-leaf parsley

400 g (14 oz) spaghetti

extra virgin olive oil

In a large heavy saucepan with a tight-fitting lid, heat half the olive oil. Add the mussels, cover, and cook briefly over a high heat until all open, about 5 minutes. Discard any still closed. Drain, retaining the liquid. When the mussels are cool remove from their shells and chop. Reduce the liquid by half, strain and add to the mussels.

In a separate large pan heat the remainder of the oil, add the garlic, chilli and oregano, and cook briefly until the garlic begins to colour. Add the wine, reduce for a minute, then add the tomatoes. Cook, stirring to prevent sticking, for 15 minutes until reduced. Add the mussels, juice, seasoning and parsley. Heat up the sauce.

Cook the spaghetti in a generous amount of boiling salted water, then drain. Add to the sauce. To serve, pour over extra virgin olive oil.

Spaghetti alle vongole
Spaghetti with clams

For 6 as a starter The smallest and sweetest clams are what you want when using them as a sauce for thin spaghetti.

3 kg (6.1/2 lb) small clams, washed
4 tablespoons extra virgin olive oil
4 garlic cloves, peeled and finely chopped
3 dried red chillies, crumbled
75 ml (2.1/2 fl oz) white wine (Sauvignon)
Maldon salt and freshly ground black pepper
1 bunch fresh flat-leaf parsley, finely chopped
400 g (14 oz) spaghetti
3 lemons, cut into quarters

Heat the olive oil in a large heavy saucepan, add the garlic and cook for a minute until just beginning to colour. Add the crumbled chilli and the clams, cover with the lid, and cook the clams over a high heat to open them, about 2-3 minutes. Remove the clams with a slotted spoon. (Discard any that have not opened.) Remove half of the clams from their shells, and discard the shells. Keep all to one side.

Add the white wine to the hot juices remaining in the pan and, keeping the heat high, reduce for 3-4 minutes. The sauce should be sweet and slightly thick. Season with pepper and some salt if necessary; the clams may be salty. Add half of the parsley and all the clams back into the sauce.

Cook the spaghetti in a generous amount of boiling salted water, then drain and add to the clam sauce. Serve with the remaining parsley and lemon quarters.

Spaghettini con calamari
Squid spaghettini

For 6 as a starter

8 medium squid, no larger than your hand
400 g (14 oz) spaghettini
Maldon salt and freshly ground black pepper
5 tablespoons olive oil
3 garlic cloves, peeled and finely chopped
3 fresh red chillies, seeded and finely chopped
75 ml (2.1/2 fl oz) white wine
1 small bunch fresh flat-leaf parsley, finely chopped

Put a large pan of salted water on to boil.

Meanwhile, clean the squid by pulling the tentacles and heads away from the bodies. Keep the tentacles together. Remove the eyes and mouth. Cut the body open so it is flat, and scrape out the guts. Slice the body into thin strips about 1 cm (1/2 in) thick. Cut the bunches of tentacles in half.

Cook the spaghettini in the boiling salted water until al dente, about 7 minutes. Remove and drain well.

Meanwhile, heat the oil in a saucepan over a high flame and quickly fry the garlic. In a matter of seconds it should begin to colour. Now add the chopped chilli and fry for a few seconds more, then add the squid strips and tentacles. Cook for about half a minute. Pour in the white wine, allow the alcohol to evaporate, and then add half the chopped parsley, and salt and black pepper.

Toss the squid sauce well with the spaghettini and serve with the rest of the parsley.

Penne con broccoli e olive verdi
Penne with broccoli and green olives

For 6 as a starter

900 g (2 lb) purple sprouting broccoli, flower heads and small leaves only
Maldon salt and freshly ground black pepper
2 small red onions, peeled and finely sliced
4 tablespoons extra virgin olive oil
2 garlic cloves, peeled and sliced
16 salted anchovy fillets, prepared (see page 346)
150 g (5 oz) pine nuts, toasted
175 g (6 oz) green olives, stoned and halved
400 g (14 oz) penne
200 g (7 oz) Pecorino cheese, grated
8 tablespoons roughly torn fresh basil

Cut the broccoli heads into small pieces, and blanch with the leaves for 5 minutes. Drain well (reserve the blanching water).

In a heavy-bottomed saucepan, gently fry the onion until golden in 2 tablespoons of the olive oil. Add the garlic and anchovy fillets, and stir to break up the anchovies; they will melt into a sauce. Add 1 ladleful of blanching water. Add the broccoli, cook for 5 minutes then add the pine nuts and olive pieces and continue to cook over a gentle heat for 5 minutes to combine all the flavours. Season.

Cook the penne in boiling salted water, then drain. Add to the sauce along with the basil, Pecorino and remaining olive oil and serve.

Penne con zucchini e ricotta
Penne with zucchini and ricotta

For 6 as a starter

1 kg (2.1/4 lb) small young zucchini
Maldon salt and freshly ground black pepper
2 tablespoons olive oil
4 garlic cloves, peeled and chopped
400 g (14 oz) penne
350 g (12 oz) ricotta cheese
1 bunch fresh basil, shredded
100 g (4 oz) Parmesan, freshly grated

Trim the zucchini, then blanch whole in boiling salted water for about 2 minutes. Drain, cool and slice at an angle, about 1 cm (1/2 in) thick.

In a large heavy saucepan heat the olive oil and cook the garlic until very soft but not brown. Add the zucchini slices and toss over a low heat for 4-5 minutes.

Cook the penne in plenty of boiling salted water, then drain well. Add to the zucchini, then crumble in the ricotta. Season, toss together and add the basil and Parmesan.

Bucatini con acciughe e pangrattato
Bucatini with anchovies and pangrattato

For 6 as a starter

8 tablespoons olive oil

3 garlic cloves, peeled and thinly sliced

3 dried red chillies, crumbled

18 salted anchovy fillets, prepared (see page 346) and roughly chopped

Maldon salt and freshly ground black pepper

zest and juice of 2 lemons

400 g (14 oz) bucatini

1 small bunch fresh flat-leaf parsley, finely chopped

Pangrattato

500 ml (17 fl oz) olive oil

10 garlic cloves, peeled and kept whole

1 ciabatta loaf, bottom crust removed, made into coarse crumbs

Make the Pangrattato. Heat the oil in a small saucepan and add the garlic. Cook over a medium heat until the garlic turns golden, then discard. Add the breadcrumbs to the pan and cook until crisp and golden. Drain on kitchen paper then season.

Heat the oil in a saucepan and gently fry the garlic until it begins to colour. Add a third of the chilli and the anchovies, and stir to combine. Remove from the heat. Add the lemon juice and black pepper.

Cook the bucatini in plenty of boiling salted water and drain. Add to the anchovy sauce. Serve on individual plates and sprinkle with lemon zest, the remaining chilli, the pangrattato, and the parsley.

Polenta in brodo di pollo con cavolo nero
Wet polenta with chicken stock and cavolo nero

For 6

250 g (9 oz) bramata polenta (organic polenta flour)

8 heads cavolo nero

Maldon salt and freshly ground black pepper

4 garlic cloves, peeled

1.25-1.5 litres (2-2.1/2 pints) Chicken Stock, well seasoned (see page 142)

200 g (7 oz) unsalted butter

150-200 g (5-7 oz) Parmesan, grated

Put a large pan of water on to boil for blanching the cavolo, and season it with salt.

Prepare the cavolo nero by removing any large discoloured or tough outer leaves. Remove the central stems and discard. Wash the leaves well, then blanch with the garlic for 5 minutes until tender. Drain and pulse-chop the cavolo and garlic in the food processor. Season.

Put the polenta in a large jug so that it can be poured in a steady stream. Bring the Chicken Stock to a simmer in a large thick-bottomed saucepan; it should come halfway up the sides of the pan. Pour the polenta into the stock slowly in a continuous stream, and, using a long-handled whisk, whisk constantly so that lumps do not form, until completely blended. The polenta will start to bubble volcanically. Reduce the heat to low and cook, stirring with a spoon to prevent a skin forming on the top, for about 40-45 minutes. The polenta is cooked when it falls away from the sides of the pan. Stir in the soft butter, the Parmesan, the cavolo nero, black pepper and some salt if needed.

Polenta con tartufi bianchi
Wet polenta with fresh white truffles

For 6

350 g (12 oz) bramata polenta (organic polenta flour)
1.75-2 litres (3-3.1/2 pints) water
Maldon salt and freshly ground black pepper
175 g (6 oz) unsalted butter, softened
200 g (7 oz) Parmesan in the piece
150-175 g (5-6 oz) white truffle, carefully brushed clean

Put the polenta flour in a large jug so that it can be poured in a steady stream. Bring the water to a boil in a large thick-bottomed saucepan; it should come halfway up the sides of the pan. Add 1 teaspoon of salt and then slowly add the polenta flour in a continuous stream, stirring with a long-handled whisk all the time (so that lumps do not form) until completely blended. The polenta will start to bubble volcanically. Reduce the heat to as low as possible and cook, stirring with a spoon to prevent a skin forming on the top, for about 40-45 minutes. The polenta is cooked when it falls away from the sides of the pan. Stir in 50 g (2 oz) of the butter and 100 g (4 oz) of the Parmesan, grated.

Divide the polenta between the plates, and season with salt and pepper. Mash the remaining butter with a spoon, and spread a little over each portion. Grate or shave the remaining Parmesan directly on top, then finally cover completely with fine shavings of white truffle, as much as you can afford: a generous helping would be about 175 g (6 oz) for six people.

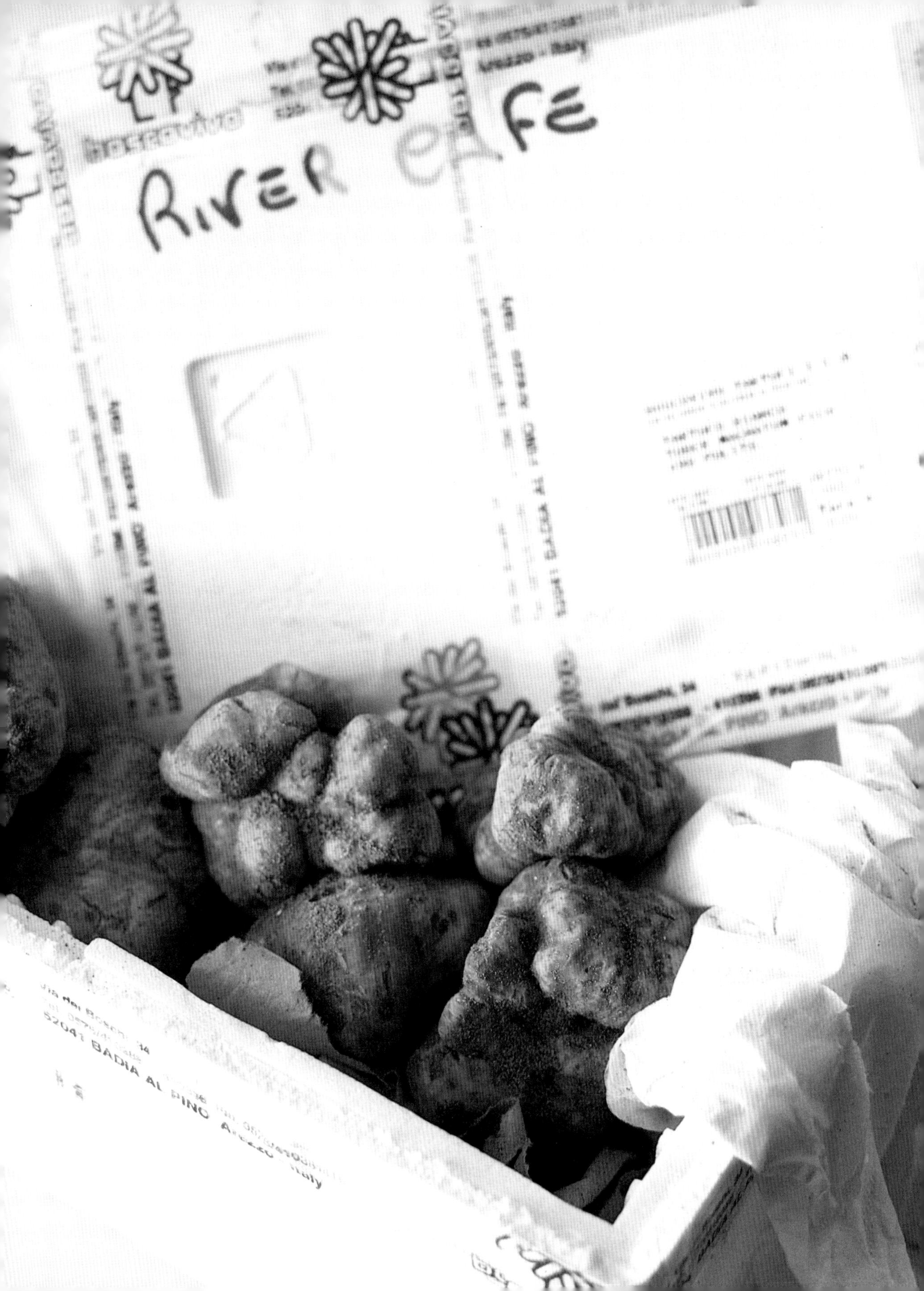
RIVER
FE
52041 BADIA AL PINO

Polenta con porcini freschi
Wet polenta with fresh porcini

For 6-8

2 kg (4.1/2 lb) fresh porcini mushrooms, brushed clean and cut into 5 cm (2 in) slices

350 g (12 oz) bramata polenta (organic polenta flour)

1.75-2 litres (3-3.1/2 pints) water

Maldon salt and freshly ground black pepper

200 g (7 oz) unsalted butter, softened

200 g (7 oz) Parmesan, grated

3 tablespoons olive oil

2 garlic cloves, peeled and thinly sliced

1 small dried red chilli, crumbled

juice of 1 lemon

4 tablespoons roughly chopped fresh flat-leaf parsley

Make the Wet Polenta as in the previous recipe. When cooked, stir in 50 g (2 oz) of the soft butter, half the grated Parmesan, black pepper and some salt if needed.

Heat the oil and the remaining butter together in a large frying pan until almost smoking. Add the mushrooms and fry quickly, turning the slices over so that they brown evenly. Add the garlic, and stir it into the mushrooms; it will cook very quickly. Season generously with the dried chilli, salt and pepper, and finally add the lemon juice and the parsley.

Serve the wet polenta with the remaining Parmesan sprinkled over each serving before you spoon over the mushrooms.

Risotto di asparagi   Risotto con ricotta e basilico   I
erbe   Risotto con funghi di bosco   Risotto al rosma
granchio Risotto con trevisano e pancetta   Risotto c

bisi   Risotto verde con pancetta   Risotto verde alle
Risotto con finocchio e vodka   Risotto con polpa di
tufi bianchi   Risotto al limone con basilico

Risotto di asparagi
Asparagus risotto

For 6

900 g (2 lb) asparagus, trimmed
1 litre (1.3/4 pints) Chicken Stock (see page 142)
Maldon salt and freshly ground black pepper
1 small red onion, peeled and very finely chopped
50 g (2 oz) unsalted butter
3 tablespoons olive oil
300 g (10 oz) risotto rice
75 ml (2.1/2 fl oz) vermouth
175 g (6 oz) Parmesan, freshly grated

Heat the Chicken Stock and check for seasoning.

Cut the tips off the asparagus and keep to one side. Chop the tender parts of the stalks into approximately 2.5 cm (1 in) pieces.

Blanch the asparagus tips for 2 minutes, then blanch the stalks for about 3 minutes. In a blender pulse the stalks with a ladle of stock.

In a heavy saucepan cook the onion in half the butter and the olive oil over a low heat for about 10 minutes until soft. Add the rice and cook gently, stirring, for 2 minutes to coat the rice with the oil. Start to add the stock, ladle by ladle, stirring constantly, allowing each ladleful to be absorbed before adding the next. Continue until the rice is al dente, usually about 20 minutes, add the stalk purée, vermouth, asparagus tips, the rest of the butter and the Parmesan.

Stir to combine and season. Serve with Parmesan.

Risotto con ricotta e basilico
Risotto with ricotta and basil

For 6

1 litre (1.3/4 pints) Chicken Stock (see page 142)
Maldon salt and freshly ground black pepper
175 g (6 oz) fresh ricotta cheese
3 tablespoons olive oil
1 medium red onion, peeled and finely chopped
300 g (10 oz) risotto rice
100 g (4 oz) fresh basil leaves, finely chopped
100 g (4 oz) Parmesan, freshly grated

Heat the Chicken Stock, and check for seasoning.

Place the ricotta in a bowl and break up into small lumps with a fork.

Heat the oil in a large saucepan over a low heat and cook the onion for about 10 minutes until soft. Add the rice and turn to coat with oil and onion. The rice should not colour, but become translucent. Start to add the hot seasoned stock, ladle by ladle, allowing each ladleful to be absorbed by the rice before adding the next. Continue cooking until the rice is al dente, usually about 20 minutes.

Lightly fold in the basil, ricotta and Parmesan. Check for seasoning and serve immediately.

Risi e bisi

For 6

3 kg (6.1/2 lb) fresh young peas in their pods

1.5 litres (2.1/2 pints) Chicken Stock (see page 142)

Maldon salt and freshly ground black pepper

4 tablespoons chopped fresh mint

100 g (4 oz) unsalted butter

2 tablespoons extra virgin olive oil

1 small red onion, peeled and finely chopped

300 g (10 oz) risotto rice

4 tablespoons chopped fresh flat-leaf parsley

150 g (5 oz) Parmesan, grated

Choose the greenest and crispest peas. Shell them and keep about half of the pods. To prepare the selected pods for dissolving into the soup, pull the sides apart and peel away the thin membrane on the inside of each side. It will come away easily if you snap off the stalk and pull the membrane slowly down the length of the pod. Trim away the stringy edges.

To start the risotto-soup, heat the Chicken Stock to a slow boil and check for seasoning. Blanch half the peas and 3 tablespoons of the mint leaves in the boiling stock. Remove using a slotted spoon, and put in a food processor with a ladle of stock. Pulse-chop to a rough purée. Set aside.

Melt the butter and oil together in a heavy-bottomed saucepan. Add the onion and fry gently until the onion begins to colour.

Add the rice and stir to coat each grain with onion, oil and butter for 3-4 minutes. Add the remaining fresh peas and chopped mint, and then the prepared pods. Stir and fry for just a minute, then add the stock, ladle by ladle, as for a regular risotto. Stir all the time, keeping the mixture very wet.

Just before the rice is al dente, add the pea purée, and stir to heat through. Then add the parsley and half the Parmesan. Season, and sprinkle with the remaining Parmesan.

Risotto verde con pancetta
Green risotto with pancetta

For 6 To make the risotto even greener, add 75 g (3 oz) blanched and pulse-chopped peas to the spinach.

500 g (18 oz) spinach, tough stalks removed
1 bunch fresh mint, leaves picked from the stalks
Maldon salt and freshly ground black pepper
1 litre (1.3/4 pints) Chicken Stock (see page 142)
100 g (4 oz) unsalted butter
1 red onion, peeled and finely chopped
300 g (10 oz) pancetta affumicata, cut into fine matchsticks
300 g (10 oz) risotto rice
75 ml (2.1/2 fl oz) extra dry white vermouth
100 g (4 oz) Pecorino cheese or Parmesan, freshly grated
freshly grated nutmeg

Wash the spinach thoroughly, then blanch with the mint in plenty of boiling salted water.

Drain the spinach and mint, cool and chop finely. We use a food processor.

Heat the Chicken Stock and check for seasoning.

In a thick-bottomed pan melt most of the butter and gently fry the chopped onion and pancetta together until the onion begins to turn golden and the pancetta becomes translucent. Add the rice and stir to coat each grain for 3-4 minutes. The rice should become translucent. Start to add the hot stock, ladle by ladle, constantly stirring, allowing each ladle to be absorbed by the rice before adding the next. Continue until the rice is al dente, usually about 20 minutes, then add the chopped spinach and mint, the remaining butter in small pieces, the vermouth and half the Pecorino or Parmesan.

Combine well. Adjust the seasoning with salt, pepper and nutmeg to taste. Serve with the remaining Pecorino or Parmesan.

Risotto verde alle erbe
Green risotto with herbs

For 6 This risotto is completely vegetarian.

1 kg (2.1/4 lb) spinach, tough stalks removed

1 bunch fresh mint, leaves picked from the stalks

Maldon salt and freshly ground black pepper

500 g (18 oz) podded peas

1 litre (1.3/4 pints) Vegetable Stock (see page 143)

100 g (4 oz) unsalted butter

2 small red onions, peeled and finely chopped

1/2 head celery, chopped (chop leaves too and set aside)

1 garlic clove, peeled and chopped

2 tablespoons chopped fresh thyme

300 g (10 oz) risotto rice

75 ml (2.1/2 fl oz) extra dry white vermouth

100 g (4 oz) Parmesan, freshly grated

3 tablespoons each of chopped fresh marjoram and basil

4 tablespoons double cream

Wash the spinach thoroughly then blanch with the mint in plenty of boiling salted water. Drain well, keeping the water. Blanch the peas in the same water, then drain. Blend the spinach, peas and mint to a rough purée in a food processor.

Heat the Vegetable Stock and check for seasoning.

In a heavy-bottomed saucepan, melt half the butter and gently fry the onion and celery until soft. Add the chopped garlic, celery leaves and thyme, stir to combine, and cook for a few minutes before adding the rice. Stir to coat each grain for a few minutes. The rice should become translucent. Add the vermouth and cook, stirring constantly, until it is absorbed. Start to add the hot stock, ladle by ladle, constantly stirring, allowing each ladle to be absorbed by the rice before adding the next. Continue until the rice is al dente, usually about 20 minutes, then add the spinach and pea purée and the remainder of the butter.

Combine the grated Parmesan with the chopped herbs and the cream. Serve the risotto with the Parmesan and herb cream stirred in.

Risotto con funghi di bosco
Wild mushroom risotto

For 6 A good mixture of wild mushrooms is best (see below). Choose whatever you can get hold of, but you need at least 750 g (a good 1.1/2 lb) in total to serve six.

at least 750 g (a good 1.1/2 lb) mixed wild mushrooms (fresh porcini, girolles, chanterelles gris, trompettes de mort)
60 g (2.1/4 oz) dried porcini, soaked for 30 minutes in hot water, drained and roughly chopped (liquid strained and reserved)
4 tablespoons olive oil
4-5 garlic cloves, peeled and finely chopped
Maldon salt and freshly ground black pepper
750 ml (15 fl oz) Chicken Stock (see page 142)
150 g (5 oz) unsalted butter
1 red onion, peeled and finely chopped
300 g (10 oz) risotto rice
200 g (7 oz) Parmesan, grated
1 bunch fresh flat-leaf parsley, leaves picked from the stalks, finely chopped

Pick through the mushrooms, removing leaves and base of stems. Clean the fresh porcini and the girolles by brushing them lightly with a dry pastry brush. Submerge the chanterelles gris and trompettes de mort briefly in cold water and wash them vigorously. Immediately drain and dry in a salad spinner. Tear any larger mushrooms into smaller pieces.

In a large heavy saucepan heat 3 tablespoons of the olive oil until smoking. Add the mushrooms to the oil in small batches. Add half the chopped garlic after a minute or two. Season and fry for a couple of minutes more until cooked.

Heat the Chicken Stock and check for seasoning.

In a heavy-bottomed pan heat half the butter with the remaining olive oil. Add the chopped onion and cook on a gentle heat until the onion is soft.

Add the dried porcini to the pan with the remaining garlic. Cook for a minute. Add the rice and stir until each grain is coated. Start adding the stock, ladle by ladle, constantly stirring, allowing each ladleful to be absorbed by the rice before adding the next. Add some of the porcini liquid to the stock for flavour, and continue until the rice is cooked al dente, usually about 20 minutes. Add the cooked wild mushrooms, the remaining butter, the Parmesan and chopped parsley. Serve immediately.

Risotto al rosmarino
Rosemary risotto

For 6

1 litre (1.3/4 pints) Chicken Stock (see page 142)
Maldon salt and freshly ground black pepper
500 g (18 oz) very ripe plum tomatoes
50 g (2 oz) unsalted butter
2 tablespoons olive oil
1 head celery, white tender parts only, finely chopped
1 small red onion, peeled and finely chopped
4 garlic cloves, peeled and finely chopped
2 branches very fresh rosemary, leaves picked from the stalks, finely chopped, plus 6
    small sprigs for serving
300 g (10 oz) risotto rice
6 teaspoons mascarpone cheese
150-200 g (5-7 oz) Parmesan, grated

Heat the Chicken Stock, and check for seasoning.

Blanch the tomatoes in boiling water for a minute, remove and place in iced water.
Skin and seed them into a sieve over a bowl to reserve the juices. Discard the seeds
and skin. Chop the tomatoes finely.

In a heavy-bottomed pan heat the butter and olive oil. Add the celery and onion and
cook on a low heat for 5 minutes; they should become soft and slightly coloured. Add
the garlic and chopped rosemary, cook for a minute, then add half of the tomato pulp.
Stir to allow the tomato to reduce for 3-4 minutes before adding the rice. Stir the rice
into the sauce to allow it to absorb the red of the tomato, cooking it for about 5

minutes. Start adding the hot stock ladle by ladle, alternating it with the reserved tomato liquid; stir constantly and allow each ladleful to be absorbed by the rice before adding the next. Add the remaining chopped tomato pulp about halfway through the cooking. Cook, stirring constantly, until the rice is al dente, usually about 20 minutes. Check for seasoning. Serve with a spoon of mascarpone, some Parmesan and a sprig of rosemary.

Risotto con finocchio e vodka
Risotto with fennel and vodka

For 6

3 fennel bulbs, with their green tops

2 garlic cloves, peeled

1.1/2 small dried red chillies

1.1/2 teaspoons fennel seeds

Maldon salt and freshly ground black pepper

250 ml (8 fl oz) vodka

juice of 1.1/2 lemons

1 litre (1.3/4 pints) Chicken Stock (see page 142)

100 g (4 oz) unsalted butter

2 tablespoons olive oil

1 small red onion, peeled and finely chopped

300 g (10 oz) risotto rice

100 g (4 oz) Parmesan, grated

Remove and discard the tough outer leaves of the fennel bulbs and finely chop the remainder of the bulbs. Chop the fennel tops and keep separately.

In a pestle and mortar crush the garlic, dried chilli and fennel seeds with 1 teaspoon Maldon salt.

In a bowl, mix the vodka, lemon juice and chopped fennel tops to allow their flavours to combine.

Heat the Chicken Stock, and check for seasoning.

Melt half the butter and the olive oil in a saucepan, then add the chopped onion.

Cook for a minute or two, keeping the heat low, then add the fennel seed paste from the mortar and let it cook briefly before adding the chopped fennel bulb. Let this cook slowly until soft. Add the rice and stir for a minute to coat each grain. Start to add the hot stock, ladle by ladle, stirring continuously, and allowing each ladleful to be absorbed by the rice before adding the next. Continue until the rice is al dente, usually about 20 minutes, then stir in the remaining butter and the vodka, fennel tops and lemon juice mixture. Sprinkle with Parmesan.

Risotto con polpa di granchio
Crab risotto

For 6

4 tablespoons olive oil

1 small red onion, peeled and finely chopped

2 small fennel bulbs, finely chopped (keep the leaves, chop and set aside)

3 garlic cloves, peeled and chopped

10 fennel seeds, crushed

2 small dried red chillies, crumbled

300 g (10 oz) risotto rice

1 x 800 g (1.3/4 lb) tin peeled plum tomatoes, drained of their juices

1.5 litres (2.1/2 pints) Fish Stock (see page 142)

Maldon salt and freshly ground black pepper

75 ml (2.1/2 fl oz) Italian oaked Chardonnay

1 x 2.25 kg (5 lb) live crab, boiled, cooled, and white and dark meats separated

juice of 2 lemons

1 bunch fresh flat-leaf parsley, roughly chopped

extra virgin olive oil

Heat the oil in a heavy-bottomed saucepan. Add the onion and fennel and fry together, stirring, over a low heat until soft and beginning to colour. Add the garlic and cook briefly, then add the fennel seeds and chilli. Stir, and as soon as the garlic turns in colour, add the rice and stir to coat. Add the drained tomatoes and break them up into the rice to allow the tomato to be absorbed before you start to add the stock. You can raise the temperature a little, but always stir to prevent sticking.

Heat the Fish Stock, and check for seasoning.

Add the Chardonnay to the rice and cook, stirring constantly, for a minute or until the wine too is absorbed. Reduce the heat and over a low flame, gently stirring, add the hot Fish Stock, ladle by ladle, constantly stirring, allowing each ladle to be absorbed by the rice before adding the next. Continue until the rice is al dente, usually about 20 minutes.

Stir in first the brown crab meat with the lemon juice, then the white meat and the parsley and fennel leaves, folding in gently, just sufficiently for the crab meats to heat through. Check for seasoning, and serve the risotto with some extra virgin olive oil on the top.

Risotto con trevisano e pancetta
Trevise and pancetta risotto

For 6 Trevise is available between December and February. True Italian trevise has long pointed leaves and is sold on the stalk, which is also delicious.

1 litre (1.3/4 pints) Chicken Stock (see page 142)
Maldon salt and freshly ground black pepper
5 heads trevise
1 red onion, peeled and finely chopped
2 celery stalks, finely chopped
150 g (5 oz) pancetta, cut into fine matchsticks
165 g (5.1/2 oz) unsalted butter
1 garlic clove, peeled and crushed
300 g (10 oz) risotto rice
150 ml (5 fl oz) Valpolicella Classico (red wine)
100 g (4 oz) Parmesan, freshly grated

Heat the Chicken Stock, and check for seasoning.

Trim the trevise, and cut the leaves from the white ribs. Chop both red and white, and keep separate.

Fry the onion, celery and pancetta in 100 g (4 oz) of the butter until the onion and celery are light gold and soft, and the pancetta has become translucent. Add the garlic and the white parts of the trevise, stir and cook for 2 minutes. Add the rice and turn to coat the rice, combining the flavours. Pour in the wine, allow it to reduce and colour the rice, then start to add the hot seasoned stock, ladle by ladle. Allow each ladleful to be absorbed by the rice before adding the next. Continue in this way until the rice is al dente, usually about 20 minutes.

In a separate saucepan heat 50 g (2 oz) of the remaining butter. Add the red part of the trevise and cook for a minute. Stir into the finished risotto, then add the remaining butter and the Parmesan.

Risotto con tartufi bianchi
White truffle risotto

For 6

1 litre (1.3/4 pints) Chicken Stock (see page 142)

Maldon salt and freshly ground black pepper

150 g (5 oz) unsalted butter

1 small red onion, peeled and finely chopped

1 head celery, white tender part only, finely chopped

300 g (10 oz) risotto rice

100 ml (3.1/2 fl oz) vermouth

150 ml (5 fl oz) double cream

1/2 nutmeg, freshly grated

175 g (6 oz) Parmesan, freshly grated

150-175 g (5-6 oz) white truffles, carefully brushed clean

Heat the Chicken Stock, and check for seasoning.

Melt half the butter in a thick-bottomed saucepan, and gently fry the onion and celery until soft and beginning to brown. Add the rice and stir to combine the rice with the vegetables and coat it with butter. The rice should become opaque. Start to add the hot stock, ladle by ladle, stirring all the time, allowing the rice to absorb each ladleful before adding the next. Add the vermouth and cream just before the rice is cooked. Season with salt, pepper and a few gratings of nutmeg. Finally stir in the remaining butter and half the Parmesan.

Serve on warm plates with the remaining Parmesan, and generously shave the truffles equally over each portion.

Risotto al limone con basilico
Lemon risotto with basil

For 6

1 litre (1.3/4 pints) Chicken Stock (see page 142)

Maldon salt and freshly ground black pepper

125 g (4.1/2 oz) unsalted butter

1 red onion, peeled and finely chopped

1 head celery, white parts only, chopped, plus leaves

1 garlic clove, peeled and chopped

300 g (10 oz) risotto rice

150 ml (5 fl oz) dry vermouth

6 tablespoons roughly chopped fresh basil

juice and zest of 4 large washed lemons

100 g (4 oz) Parmesan, freshly grated

5 tablespoons mascarpone cheese

Heat the Chicken Stock, and check for seasoning.

Melt half the butter in a thick-bottomed saucepan. Gently fry the onion and celery stalk until soft. Add the garlic and celery leaves, stir to combine, then add the rice. Stir the rice to coat then add the vermouth. Allow it to bubble and reduce, then add the hot stock ladle by ladle over a gentle heat. Stir constantly and allow each ladleful to be absorbed before adding another.

When the rice is al dente, usually after about 20 minutes, stir in most of the basil, the lemon juice and zest, half the Parmesan and the mascarpone. Stir once; the texture should be creamy. Serve with a few basil leaves and the remaining Parmesan.

Sou
Stoc

os
ks
5

Ribollita d'estiva   Acquacotta di primavera   Acquac
Zuppa di fave fresche   Zuppa di cannellini e cicoria
Brodo di finocchio e ricotta   Brodo de pesce   Brodo di

Zuppa di castagne, zucca e farro   Zuppa lombarda
a di rucola e patate   Zuppa di baccalà   Zuppa di farro
● Brodo di verdura   Zuppa di orzo

Ribollita d'estiva
Summer ribollita

For 8

500 g (18 oz) fresh borlotti (or cannellini) beans, podded weight, cooked (see
  page 346)

extra virgin olive oil

4 young onions, red or white, peeled and chopped

1 head celery, plus leaves, stalks chopped

1 head fresh garlic, peeled and sliced

500 g (18 oz) Swiss chard stalks and leaves, stalks sliced into large matchsticks

1 bunch fresh basil, leaves picked from the stalks

1 bunch fresh mint, leaves picked from the stalks

1 bunch fresh marjoram, leaves picked from the stalks

1 bunch fresh flat-leaf parsley, leaves picked from the stalks

2 kg (4.1/2 lb) fresh ripe plum tomatoes, skinned, seeded and chopped

Maldon salt and freshly ground black pepper

1 bunch fresh borage (optional)

300 g (10 oz) fresh spinach, tough stalks removed

2 loaves ciabatta bread, stale if possible, crusts removed

1 fresh red chilli

In a large heavy pan heat 3 tablespoons of olive oil, then add the onion and celery stalks. Stir and cook gently until they soften and brown. Add the garlic and chard stalks and continue to cook. When the garlic begins to colour, add half the basil, mint, marjoram, parsley and celery leaves. Gently fry and stir together to combine the herbs, then add the chopped tomatoes. Season and simmer for 30 minutes: the tomatoes should reduce with the vegetables.

Separately, in another large saucepan full of boiling water with plenty of salt, blanch the borage and chard leaves and then the spinach. Drain, keeping the blanching water, and roughly chop. Add the leaves to the vegetable and tomato mixture along with the cooked beans. Tear up the ciabatta into 3-5 cm (1-2 in) lengths and add to the soup. Pour over some of the blanching water to moisten the bread, and stir in the remaining herbs. Check for seasoning, then add salt and pepper to taste and 3 tablespoons olive oil. The consistency should be very thick.

Get rid of the seeds and fibres from the inside of the red chilli by cutting it in half and scraping with a teaspoon. Chop the chilli roughly, then place in a small bowl and add 2 tablespoons extra virgin olive oil. To serve, dribble this chilli sauce over each bowl of soup when serving.

Acquacotta di primavera
Spring acquacotta

For 6

300 g (10 oz) sprue asparagus

6 small artichoke hearts (see page 172)

zest and juice of 1 lemon

400 g (14 oz) Swiss chard

300 g (10 oz) podded fresh peas

300 g (10 oz) podded fresh young broad beans

2 tablespoons olive oil

3 garlic cloves, peeled and finely chopped

Maldon salt and freshly ground black pepper

2 tablespoons each of chopped fresh parsley, basil and thyme

6 crostini (see page 290)

Cut off and discard the hard part of the asparagus stalks. Slice each artichoke heart into four and put in a bowl of water with the lemon juice. Separate the stalks from the leaves of the chard. Cut the stalks into 5 mm (1/4 in) pieces, and roughly chop the leaves.

In a saucepan, heat the oil and fry the garlic until golden. Add the artichokes. After 2 minutes add the chard stalks and cook together until soft and beginning to colour.

Add half the peas, broad beans and chard leaves, season and just cover with boiling water. Cook over a moderate heat for 20 minutes. Add the remaining vegetables and cook for a further 5 minutes. Add the lemon zest and the herbs at the last moment and serve with a crostini in each soup bowl.

Acquacotta

For 6-8

75 g (3 oz) dried funghi porcini
2 red onions, peeled
1 head celery
2 carrots, peeled
4 garlic cloves, peeled
3 tablespoons olive oil
1 small bunch fresh thyme
1/2 bunch fresh parsley
2 small dried red chillies, crumbled
1 x 1.85 kg (4.1/4 lb) tin peeled plum tomatoes, plus their juices
Maldon salt and freshly ground black pepper
6 crostini (see page 290)
extra virgin olive oil
100 g (4 oz) Parmesan, freshly grated

Place the porcini in a bowl and pour boiling water over them. Leave for 15 minutes.

Roughly chop the onions. Remove and discard the tough outer stalks from the celery, and cut the tender heart and green leaves into small pieces. Cut the carrots roughly into 1 cm (1/2 in) slices. Slice the garlic finely.

Heat the oil in a large heavy-bottomed saucepan and gently fry the onion with the celery and carrot until soft and lightly coloured. Add the thyme, garlic, parsley and chilli, and continue to fry, stirring to combine the flavours. The longer you cook at this stage, the better the flavour of the soup will be.

Drain the porcini, keeping the soaking liquid, and add the porcini to the onion and celery. Fry together for a few minutes, then add the tomatoes (but not the juice), one by one. Break them up with a spoon and stir into the onion mixture. When the tomatoes have begun to thicken – this will take about 30-45 minutes – add a little of the tomato juice and the strained reserved porcini water. Stir and cook together gently for about another 30 minutes. Your soup should be thick. Season with salt and pepper.

Place a crostini in each soup bowl, then ladle in the soup. Drizzle with extra virgin olive oil and sprinkle with Parmesan.

Zuppa di castagne, zucca e farro
Chestnut, pumpkin and farro soup

For 6

1 kg (2.1/4 lb) fresh chestnuts, boiled, peeled and roughly chopped
1 kg (2.1/4 lb) pumpkin flesh, roasted and roughly chopped (see page 158)
150 g (5 oz) farro, soaked in cold water for 1.1/2 hours
100 ml (3 1/2 fl oz) olive oil
1 red onion, peeled and finely chopped
1 head celery, roughly chopped
150 g (5 oz) pancetta affumicata, finely diced
5 garlic cloves, peeled and chopped
50 g (2 oz) fresh rosemary, chopped
2 dried red chillies, crumbled
1 litre (1.3/4 pints) Chicken Stock (see page 142)
Maldon salt and freshly ground black pepper
extra virgin olive oil

Drain the farro, then put in a pan, cover with cold water, and bring to the boil. Cook until the faro expands and is al dente, about 20 minutes.

Meanwhile, in a heavy saucepan large enough to hold the soup, heat 3 tablespoons of the olive oil. Add the onion and celery, fry gently to soften, then add the pancetta, garlic, chopped rosemary and chilli. Allow this to cook on a low heat until the pancetta and garlic begin to colour, then add the chestnuts. Let them absorb the pancetta flavours, about 5 minutes, then add the pumpkin. Cook this for a further 5 minutes, then add the warmed Chicken Stock. Finally add the cooked farro. Heat through, check for seasoning, then serve, drizzled with extra virgin olive oil.

Zuppa lombarda
Broth with cannellini beans and ciabatta

For 6 It is essential to make the broth for this soup yourself with the best organic chicken you can find.

2 litres (3.1/2 pints) Chicken Stock (see page 142)
200 g (7 oz) dried cannellini beans, soaked overnight and cooked (see page 346)
Maldon salt and freshly ground black pepper
12 crostini, sliced very thinly (see page 290)
extra virgin olive oil

Heat the cooked cannellini beans, then take out 300 ml (10 fl oz) of them, plus their cooking water, and purée to a cream in the food processor. Return to the whole beans.

Skim off any chicken fat from the surface of the broth. Season the broth to taste with salt and pepper. It should be sweet and clear. Heat.

Place 2 crostini in each soup bowl, then pour over the hot broth. Top with 3 tablespoons of cooked cannellini beans and the liquid they cooked in. Serve drizzled with extra virgin olive oil.

Zuppa di fave fresche
Fresh broad bean soup

For 6

3 kg (6.1/2 lb) very young broad beans, podded
1.5 kg (3.1/4 lb) very young peas, podded
2 tablespoons olive oil
1 red onion, peeled and finely sliced
2 medium potatoes, peeled and sliced
1 bunch fresh mint, leaves removed from the stalks (retain the stalks)
water or Chicken Stock (see page 142)
Maldon salt and freshly ground black pepper
3 tablespoons chopped fresh mint

Heat the olive oil in a thick-bottomed pan, and gently fry the onion until soft and translucent. Add the peas and potatoes, and cook, stirring, for 5 minutes then add a handful of the mint. Pour in enough stock or water to cover, and simmer for 15 minutes. Add half the broad beans after 5 minutes.

In a separate pan boil 2 litres (3.1/2 pints) water. Add the mint stalks and the remaining beans. Cook covered, for 2-3 minutes. Drain, and discard the stalks.

Put a ladle of the soup mixture in the food processor with a ladle of blanched broad beans, and pulse-chop. Keep to one side. Pulse-chop the remainder of the soup with the rest of the mint leaves. Return to the pan. Add the remaining whole broad beans and the puréed broad beans, and season the soup well with salt and pepper.

Reheat gently and serve with the chopped fresh mint. The soup should be very thick with a combination of whole young broad beans and a rough purée.

Zuppa di cannellini e cicoria
Cannellini bean and bitter cicoria soup

For 6 Bitter cicoria is a cultivated dandelion leaf grown in Italy.

250 g (9 oz) dried cannellini beans, soaked and cooked (see page 346)
1 kg (2.1/4 lb) cicoria
Maldon salt and freshly ground black pepper
extra virgin olive oil
2 garlic cloves, peeled and chopped
1 dried red chilli, crumbled

Cook the cannellini beans as described on page 346, then leave to rest in their cooking water.

Prepare the cicoria. Strip the green from the thick stems where they are tough and stringy and cut into pieces about 2 cm (3/4 in) in length. Blanch in a large saucepan of boiling salted water. Remove and refresh under cold water, then drain well and chop coarsely.

Heat 2 tablespoons olive oil in a large pan and cook the garlic lightly until soft, then add the cicoria pieces. Cook for a minute, then add salt, pepper and the chilli.

Drain the cannellini beans, reserving their liquid, and stir into the cicoria mixture. Put three-quarters of this into a food processor with a little of the bean liquid, and briefly pulse. If it is too thick to mix, add more liquid. Return the mixture to the pan with the whole beans, and mix together. Season with salt, pepper and more chilli according to taste. Add more liquid if necessary, but this is meant to be a very thick soup.

Serve with a generous amount of extra virgin olive oil.

Zuppa di rucola e patate
Rocket and potato soup

For 6

1 kg (2.1/4 lb) potatoes (Linska or Roseval), peeled and cut into 1 cm (1/2 in) dice
1 kg (2.1/4 lb) rocket, tough stalks removed, leaves roughly chopped
1.5 litres (2.1/2 pints) Chicken Stock (see page 142), well seasoned
Maldon salt and freshly ground black pepper
olive oil
3 garlic cloves, peeled and chopped
2 dried red chillies, crumbled
3 tablespoons roughly chopped fresh parsley
6 crostini (see page 290)
freshly grated Parmesan
1 fresh red chilli, seeded, chopped and marinated in 2 tablespoons olive oil

Heat the Chicken Stock and check it for seasoning.

In a large heavy-bottomed saucepan, heat 2 tablespoons olive oil and gently fry the garlic until golden. Add the chilli and potatoes and stir-fry for a few minutes. Add the parsley and half the rocket and cook for just a few seconds. Add about 3 ladlefuls of the hot stock. Simmer on a medium heat, stirring quite frequently, for about 20 minutes. The potatoes should break up into the stock, but small pieces will remain. Put the remainder of the stock into a liquidiser and add most of the rest of the rocket. Pulse together, then stir this liquid into the soup. Check for seasoning.

Place a crostini in each bowl, then add a tablespoon of fresh rocket leaves and a tablespoon of Parmesan. Ladle over the hot soup. Serve with a teaspoon of chilli oil.

Zuppa di baccalà

Salt cod soup

For 6

1 kg (2.1/4 lb) salt cod (baccalà), soaked (see page 212)

4 tablespoons olive oil

1 medium red onion, peeled and finely sliced

1/2 head celery, plus leaves, stalks finely sliced

3 garlic cloves, peeled and finely sliced

2 tablespoons chopped fresh thyme

3 bay leaves

1 teaspoon fennel seeds, crushed

2 small dried red chillies, crumbled

6 ripe plum tomatoes, skinned, seeded and chopped

150 ml (5 fl oz) dry white wine

6 small potatoes, peeled and cut into quarters

freshly ground black pepper

4 tablespoons chopped fresh flat-leaf parsley

6 crostini (see page 290)

2 fresh red chillies, first finger size, seeded and chopped

extra virgin olive oil

Cut the salt cod into 10 cm (4 in) pieces.

Heat the olive oil in a thick-bottomed pan and fry the onion for a minute until softened, then add the celery stalks, leaves and garlic, and cook until slightly coloured. Now add the thyme, bay leaves, crushed fennel seeds and dried chilli. Stir for a second just to combine, then add the tomatoes. Push the tomatoes into the onion mixture to break up any pieces, and stir. As soon as the tomatoes become sticky, add the wine, potatoes and enough water to cover. Cook, stirring frequently, until the potatoes are al dente.

Add the cod, lower the heat, and simmer, covered, for 15-20 minutes. The cod should be tender and just beginning to break up. Add pepper to taste and most of the parsley.

Place one crostini in each soup bowl, pour over the broth and pieces of cod, and sprinkle with the remainder of the parsley and a little fresh chilli. Serve drizzled with extra virgin olive oil.

Zuppa di farro
Soup of farro, borlotti, cannellini and chickpeas

For 6

200 g (7 oz) farro, soaked in salted water for 2 hours
100 g (4 oz) dried borlotti beans, cooked (see page 346), cooking liquid retained
100 g (4 oz) cannellini beans, cooked (see page 346), cooking liquid retained
75 g (3 oz) chickpeas, cooked (see page 214)
3 tablespoons olive oil
3 garlic cloves, peeled and coarsely sliced
1 x 800 g (1.3/4 lb) tin peeled plum tomatoes
3 sprigs fresh rosemary, chopped
Maldon salt and freshly ground black pepper
6 crostini (see page 290)
extra virgin olive oil

Drain the farro. Put in a saucepan, cover and bring to the boil. Reduce the heat and simmer for 45 minutes or until al dente.

Heat 1 tablespoon of the oil in a thick-bottomed pan, and fry 1 garlic clove until soft. Add the tomatoes and their juices, and cook, stirring, over a moderate heat for half an hour. Season and set aside.

Heat the remaining olive oil in a large pan, and add the remaining garlic and rosemary. When the garlic begins to colour, add the tomato sauce and stir. Add the beans and their cooking liquid and the drained chickpeas, bring to a boil, and add the farro. Cook for a further 15 minutes then season.

Place a crostini in each soup bowl and ladle the soup over. Drizzle with olive oil.

Brodo di finochio e ricotta
Sardinian wild fennel soup

For 6

4 medium fennel bulbs, with leaves
1.5 litres (2.1/2 pints) Chicken Stock (see page 142)
Maldon salt and freshly ground black pepper
6 crostini (see page 290)
250 g (9 oz) ricotta cheese
extra virgin olive oil
150 g (5 oz) Parmesan, freshly grated

Slice the fine leaves from the top of the fennel and set aside. Remove the tough or bruised outside layer of the fennel and trim the base. With the base on the board, stand the fennel up, and slice down, making pieces about 1 cm (1/2 in) thick.

Bring the Chicken Stock to the boil and add the fennel pieces. Cook until very tender, about 20 minutes. Add the fennel leaves and season with salt and pepper.

Place a crostini in each soup bowl. Cut the ricotta into thin slices and place on top of the crostini. Spoon over the cooked fennel pieces, then ladle in some of the stock. Drizzle olive oil over each bowl then sprinkle with the Parmesan.

Brodo di pesce
Fish stock

Makes 1.5 litres (2.1/2 pints) This is the stock to use for the risotto on page 112.

heads and bones of 1-2 large turbot
1 piece sea bass or head
a handful each of fennel and parsley stalks
1 whole head garlic
1/2 head celery with leaves
2 large plum tomatoes
1/2 tablespoon each of fennel seeds,
    coriander seeds and white peppercorns
1 large branch fresh bay leaves
2 dried red chillies
150 ml (5 fl oz) dry white wine
1.75 litres (3 pints) cold water
Maldon salt

Put all the ingredients, apart from the salt, into a large pan and bring to the boil, skimming off any scum if necessary. Lower the heat and simmer very gently for about 30 minutes. Strain and use immediately, seasoning to taste with salt.

Brodo di pollo
Chicken stock

Makes 2 litres (3.1/2 pints) In a perfect world – i.e. in Bologna for instance – the stock would include a veal bone, a beef shin and a piece of pancetta.

1 x 1.5-2 kg (3.1/4-4.1/2 lb) free-range
    chicken, all fatty parts removed
1 head celery, white parts only, washed
2 large carrots, scrubbed
1 small red onion, peeled
2 tomatoes
1 head garlic, unpeeled
5 bay leaves
3 sprigs fresh thyme
1 teaspoon black peppercorns
3 litres (5 pints) cold water
Maldon salt

Put the chicken and the rest of the ingredients, apart from the salt, into a large saucepan, and bring gently to the boil. Turn the heat down and skim, then gently simmer for about 1 hour. Remove the chicken and strain out the vegetables and herbs. Season the broth

Brodo di verdura
Vegetable stock

Makes 2 litres (3.1/2 pints)

2 tablespoons olive oil

2 small red onions, peeled and roughly
   sliced

4 carrots, washed and halved

1 head celery, stalks and leaves, cut
   lengthways into four

4 leeks, tough green tops removed, halved

2 fennel bulbs, each cut into four

2 dried red chillies

4 garlic cloves, peeled

1 bunch fresh thyme

1 bunch flat-leaf parsley, leaves picked from
   the stalks (retain both)

2 litres (3.1/2 pints) water

4 bay leaves

2 tablespoons white or black peppercorns

juice of 1 lemon

Maldon salt

Heat the oil in a large heavy-bottomed saucepan, then gently fry the onion until soft. Add the carrot, celery, leek and fennel, and fry, stirring, until lightly browned. Add the chilli, garlic, thyme and parsley leaves, stir to combine and continue to cook. Add the water, parsley stalks, bay leaves and peppercorns, and bring to the boil. Lower the heat and simmer gently for about 1 hour before straining. Add the lemon juice and adjust the seasoning.

Zuppa di orzo
Barley soup

For 6

400 g (14 oz) barley, soaked in hot water for 45 minutes

3 tablespoons olive oil

1 head celery, tender stalks and young leaves separated and roughly chopped

1 red onion, peeled and chopped

1 fennel bulb, chopped, green herb parts chopped separately

3 leeks, white parts no thicker than your thumb, chopped

2 garlic cloves, peeled and finely chopped

2 small dried red chillies, crumbled

2 tablespoons each chopped fresh flat-leaf parsley and mint

4 fresh ripe tomatoes, skinned, seeded and chopped

2 litres (3.1/2 pints) Chicken Stock (see page 142)

Maldon salt and freshly ground black pepper

extra virgin olive oil (peppery new season estate-bottled is the best)

Heat the oil in a heavy saucepan then add the celery and onion and cook together until they begin to soften. Add the fennel bulb and leek and fry, stirring, until they begin to caramelise, about 15 minutes. Add the garlic and chilli, then, after 1 minute, the herbs, celery leaves and tomatoes. Stir to combine and slightly reduce, then add half the barley. Allow to absorb the flavours, then add half the Chicken Stock. Reduce the heat and cook until the barley is tender, about 30-40 minutes.

Cook the remaining barley in the rest of the stock for 30-40 minutes. Purée in a food processor and add to the soup. Season and serve with new oil. This soup should be thick and creamy.

Wood-r
Vegeta

oasted
oles

6

Zucchini al forno   Asparagi al forno   Pomidorini al
Barbe rosse in cartoccio   Barbe rosse intere al forno
Sedano rapa al forno   Trevisano con pancetta e rosm
freschi al forno   Carciofi in cartoccio con timo   Biet
con parmigiano   Patate e acciughe al forno

Zucchini al forno
Wood-roasted zucchini

For 6

18 small zucchini, trimmed and cut in half lengthways
3 garlic cloves, peeled and roughly chopped
Maldon salt and freshly ground black pepper
4 teaspoons coriander seeds
olive oil
1 bunch fresh thyme, leaves picked from the stalks

Preheat the oven to 220° C/425° F/Gas 7.

Pound the garlic, a little salt and the coriander seeds together until crushed.

Arrange the zucchini cut side up in an oiled roasting pan. Sprinkle the garlic mixture and thyme leaves loosely all over. Lightly drizzle with olive oil, and season well.

Roast the zucchini in the preheated oven for about 15 minutes until golden and cooked through.

Asparagi al forno
Wood-roasted asparagus

For 6

1.6 kg (3.1/2 lb) asparagus
olive oil
1 bunch fresh basil, leaves picked from their stalks, roughly chopped
Maldon salt and freshly ground black pepper
1 garlic clove, peeled and finely chopped
100 g (4 oz) stoned Niçoise olives

Preheat the oven to 220° C/425° F/Gas 7.

Trim the asparagus of any woody stalks by gently flexing the base of the stem until it snaps. Discard the woody ends, and wash the green stalks and tips. Dry well and place in a mixing bowl. Toss with enough olive oil to lightly coat each stalk. Add the basil, salt, pepper and garlic, and gently mix.

Arrange in an oiled roasting pan and season again. Add the olives.

Roast in the preheated oven for about 10 minutes or until the stalks are wilted and light gold in colour.

Pomidorini al forno
Wood-roasted cherry vine tomatoes

For 6

1.5 kg (3.1/4 lb) cherry tomatoes, on the vine, in about 10 small clusters
3 tablespoons olive oil
1 bunch fresh thyme in small sprigs
3 garlic cloves, peeled and thinly sliced
Maldon salt and freshly ground black pepper

Preheat the oven to 200° C/400° F/Gas 6. Place the tomatoes in an oiled roasting pan. Scatter with the thyme and garlic. Drizzle with oil, and season. Roast for 20 minutes.

Melanzane al forno
Wood-roasted aubergine

For 6

3 aubergines, sliced into discs about 2 cm (3/4 in) thick
olive oil
2 tablespoons dried oregano
2 garlic cloves, peeled and finely chopped
Maldon salt and freshly ground black pepper

Preheat the oven to 220° C/425° F/Gas 7. Lightly brush both sides of the aubergine slices with oil and place flat in a baking dish. Scatter with half the oregano and garlic and season. Bake for about 15 minutes. Turn over, sprinkle with the remaining oregano and garlic and more salt and pepper, and bake for another 5-10 minutes.

Cipolle rosse ripiene di timo
Baked red onions with thyme

For 6

12 small red onions, skins left on
4 garlic cloves, peeled and thinly sliced
1 bunch fresh thyme, leaves of 2 sprigs picked from the stalks
175 g (6 oz) unsalted butter, softened
Maldon salt and freshly ground black pepper
150-175 ml (5-6 fl oz) balsamic vinegar
150 ml (5 fl oz) red wine

Preheat the oven to 180° C/350° F/Gas 4.

Trim the base of each onion, so that they can stand. Cut a deep cross in from the top, about halfway down the height of the onion. Stand the onions in a baking dish and place a couple of slivers of garlic and a small sprig of the thyme in the incisions. Mix the butter with the remaining thyme leaves, salt and pepper, and put a teaspoonful on top of each onion. Drizzle the balsamic vinegar and red wine over the onions and season again. Cover with foil and bake in the preheated oven for about 40 minutes or until the onions have softened.

Remove the foil and reduce the oven temperature to 150° C/300° F/Gas 2, and continue to cook for another hour, basting frequently. To prevent the balsamic juices from drying up and burning, add 300 ml (10 fl oz) or so of water, or more red wine. Alternatively the temperature can be reduced to 120° C/250° F/Gas 1/2, and the onions can be roasted for longer. The onions are ready when they are soft and caramelised.

Barbe rosse in cartoccio
Baby beetroots baked in foil

For 6

18 small summer beetroots
100 ml (3.1/2 fl oz) extra virgin olive oil
Maldon salt and freshly ground black pepper
3 garlic cloves, peeled and thinly sliced
1 large bunch fresh thyme, leaves picked from the stalks
lemon juice from 2 lemons

Preheat the oven to 220° C/425° F/Gas 7.

Prepare the beetroots as in the recipe overleaf, but cutting the leaves off 5 cm (2 in) from the bulbs.

Cut foil into 18 x 13 cm (7 x 5 in) squares, or squares large enough to individually wrap each beetroot. Brush one side of the foil with olive oil. Scatter with salt and pepper, a few slices of garlic and some thyme leaves. Place the beetroots on top and wrap carefully.

Place the parcels on a baking tray and bake in the preheated oven for 45 minutes. Test by inserting the point of a knife; they should be soft.

Serve drizzled with extra virgin oil and lemon juice.

Barbe rosse intere al forno
Whole wood-roasted beetroots

For 6 Buy small beetroots roughly the size of golfballs with their leaves on and root tail intact.

18 small summer beetroots

1 bunch fresh thyme

4 garlic cloves, peeled and finely chopped

6 tablespoons extra virgin olive oil

3 tablespoons vinegar (balsamic or herb wine vinegar)

juice of 1 lemon

2 tablespoons Maldon salt

1 tablespoon freshly ground black pepper

Preheat the oven to 220° C/425° F/Gas 7.

Remove the beetroot leaves 3 cm (1.1/4 in) from the bulb, and put to one side (use them in the recipes on pages 42 and 60). Keep the root tail of the beetroots intact. Wash the beetroots thoroughly, dry, then put in a bowl.

Pull the leaves from the majority of the thyme stalks. Keep a few stalks whole.

Mix the garlic and thyme leaves and stalks with the olive oil, vinegar and lemon juice, add the seasonings, and then pour over the beetroots. Turn over and over in the marinade, and then place in a baking dish. Bake for 20 minutes. Turn the beetroots over then bake for a further 20 minutes or until cooked.

Serve warm with other wood-roasted vegetables or cold with ricotta (see page 42).

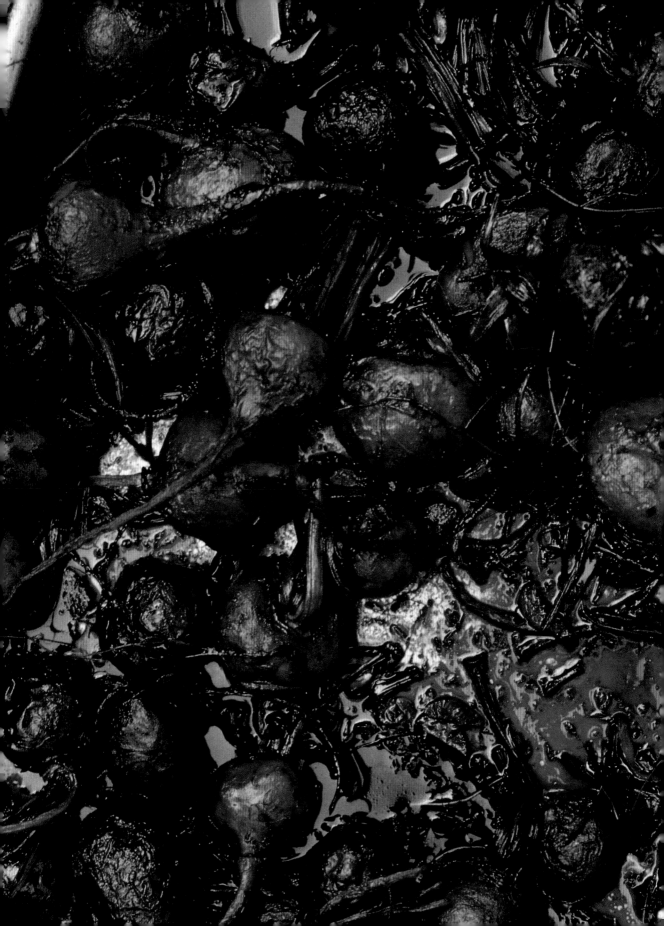

Carote intere al forno
Wood-roasted whole organic carrots

For 6

12 medium to large organic carrots, scrubbed and trimmed
2 tablespoons thyme leaves
2 garlic cloves, peeled
2 tablespoons Maldon salt and 1 tablespoon freshly ground black pepper
6 tablespoons olive oil
3 tablespoons herb wine vinegar (Volpaia 'Erbe')

Preheat oven to 220° C/425° F/Gas 7. Pound together the thyme, garlic, salt and pepper. Add the oil and vinegar. Pour over the carrots in a baking tray and toss. Roast for 35-40 minutes, turning after 20 minutes.

Zucca al forno
Wood-roasted pumpkin

For 6

1 small pumpkin, about 1 kg (2.1/2 lb), peeled, cut into wedges 2 cm (3/4 in) thick
150 ml (5 fl oz) olive oil
3 garlic cloves, peeled and finely chopped
1 small dried red chilli, crumbled
1 bunch fresh thyme, leaves picked from the stalks
Maldon salt and freshly ground black pepper

Preheat the oven to 200° C/400° F/Gas 6. Put the pumpkin pieces in a bowl with the other ingredients. Mix thoroughly to coat. Put in an oiled baking dish and roast for about an hour.

Topinambur al forno
Wood-roasted jerusalem artichokes

For 6 Roast sweet potatoes in the same way.

20 Jerusalem artichokes, peeled
100 ml (3.1/2 fl oz) olive oil
1 small bunch fresh thyme, leaves picked from the stalks
3 garlic cloves, peeled and finely chopped
Maldon salt and freshly ground black pepper

Preheat the oven to 220° C/425° F/Gas 7. Put the artichokes in a bowl with the other ingredients. Mix thoroughly. Place in an oiled baking dish and roast for about 25 minutes.

Sedano rapa al forno
Wood-roasted celeriac

For 6

2 celeriac, about 450 g (1 lb) each, peeled and cut into wedges 2 cm (3/4 in) thick
1 small bunch fresh thyme, leaves picked from the stalks
100 ml (3.1/2 fl oz) olive oil
1 head garlic, separated into cloves, peeled and chopped
Maldon salt and freshly ground black pepper

Preheat the oven to 220° C/425° F/Gas 7. Put the celeriac in a bowl with the other ingredients. Mix thoroughly. Place in an oiled baking dish and cover loosely with foil. Bake for 10 minutes. Remove the foil, turn the pieces over and roast for 20 minutes.

Trevisano con pancetta e rosmarino
Baked trevise wrapped in pancetta

For 6

6 heads trevise

24 small sprigs fresh rosemary

4 garlic cloves, peeled and sliced

Maldon salt and freshly ground black pepper

24 thin slices pancetta affumicata, about 200 g (7 oz)

extra virgin olive oil

Preheat the oven to 200° C/400° F/Gas 6.

Prepare the trevise by cutting each head into quarters lengthways so the leaves stay attached to the stem. Tuck a sprig of rosemary and a couple of garlic slices into each trevise quarter, on the cut side, and season with salt and pepper. Wrap a piece of pancetta around each quarter of trevise, tucking it in to prevent it falling off.

Place the wrapped trevise pieces in a lightly oiled baking dish, drizzle with olive oil and bake in the preheated oven until the trevise stem is tender and the pancetta is crisp, about 10-15 minutes.

Porcini al forno
Wood-roasted whole porcini

For 6

6 large whole fresh porcini, stalks attached, weighing about 200-250 g (7-9 oz) each
12 large sprigs fresh thyme
18 thin slices smoked pancetta
3 garlic cloves, peeled and finely sliced
Maldon salt and freshly ground black pepper
extra virgin olive oil
3 lemons
a handful of rocket leaves

Preheat the oven to 230° C/450° F/Gas 8.

With a soft dry brush, clean each mushroom carefully. With a sharp knife make two cuts up the length of the stalk, dividing it equally into three parts, making sure it does not become separated from its cap. In each cut place a sprig of thyme, a slice of pancetta and a few slices of garlic. Season generously, then wind a slice of pancetta round each stem to hold in the stuffing.

Heat a suitable roasting pan until hot, then add 3 tablespoons olive oil. Place the porcini in the oil and put in the oven to bake. They take from 5-15 minutes according to the size and thickness of the cap. When ready, the cap will have browned and shrunk, the stem will have coloured, and the pancetta will be cooked.

Remove the pan from the oven, and squeeze the juice of 1/2 a lemon over each porcini. Serve with the rocket leaves dressed with oil and extra lemon juice.

Cannellini secchi al forno
Baked dried cannellini beans

For 6

300 g (10 oz) dried cannellini beans
1 tablespoon bicarbonate of soda
1 head garlic
a handful of fresh sage leaves
6 tablespoons extra virgin olive oil
Maldon salt and freshly ground black pepper

Soak the beans overnight in a generous amount of water with the bicarbonate of soda.

Preheat the oven to 200° C/400° F/Gas 6.

Drain the beans well and place them in a baking dish. Add the garlic, sage, and enough water to come three-quarters up the sides of the baking dish. Pour in the olive oil to cover the beans. Cover the dish with foil and make a small hole in the centre with the point of a knife to allow steam to escape.

Place the casserole in the preheated oven and cook until the beans are very tender, about 45 minutes – although the cooking time will vary according to the quality of the beans. The liquid will evaporate, and the beans will become very tender. Season generously with salt and black pepper.

Borlotti freschi al forno
Baked fresh borlotti beans

For 6 You can cook fresh or dried borlotti beans in this way. The fresh will obviously take less time.

2 kg (4.1/2 lb) fresh borlotti beans, podded
3 large tomatoes
1 whole garlic clove with its skin
1 bunch fresh sage
120 ml (4 fl oz) extra virgin olive oil
Maldon salt and freshly ground black pepper

Preheat the oven to 200° C/400° F/Gas 6.

Choose a saucepan or casserole that you can put in your oven. The size of the pan is important; the beans should fill it to halfway up the sides. Put in the beans, whole tomatoes, garlic and sage, and pour in cold water just to come within 5 mm (1/4 in) of the top of the beans. Pour in the olive oil, or enough to cover the surface of the beans by about 1 cm (1/2 in). Seal tightly with foil, and make a hole in the middle with the point of a knife to allow steam to escape.

Place the beans in the preheated oven and bake for 3/4-1 hour. The water evaporates during cooking, and the beans will soak up the olive oil, becoming creamy and soft. Season generously with salt and black pepper.

If you have an Aga or wood oven, the beans can be cooked in the cooler oven overnight.

When serving, add a little green, fruity extra virgin olive oil.

Carciofi in cartoccio con timo
Artichokes baked in foil with thyme

For 6

12 small globe artichokes with stalks
1/2 lemon
4 garlic cloves, peeled and thinly sliced
1 bunch fresh thyme, in sprigs
Maldon salt and freshly ground black pepper
olive oil

Preheat the oven to 220° C/425° F/Gas 7.

Prepare the artichokes by first trimming the stalks, leaving about 5 cm (2 in). Peel each stalk down to the paler core. Next break off the tough outer leaves until only the pale tender leaves remain. Trim about 1 cm (1/2 in) off the top. Open the leaves and with a spoon gouge out the choke. If the artichokes are very tender this is not necessary. Rub the lemon over each artichoke to prevent discolouring.

Put a couple of slivers of garlic, a sprig of thyme and generous salt and pepper into the small cavity in each artichoke. Lay each artichoke on a piece of foil large enough to wrap tightly all around. Drizzle oil over each and season with more salt and pepper. Wrap up tightly in the foil. Roast in the preheated oven for about 30 minutes, or until tender.

Bietola gratinata
Swiss chard gratin

For 6 We adapted this recipe from one published by Lesley Forbes.

1.5 kg (3.1/4 lb) Swiss chard, leaves and their stalks separated

Maldon salt and freshly ground black pepper

50 ml (2 fl oz) herb vinegar (Volpaia 'Erbe')

3 bay leaves

1 bunch fresh thyme, leaves picked from 1/2 the stalks

100 g (4 oz) unsalted butter

1 red onion, peeled and sliced

2 garlic cloves, peeled and finely sliced

1 dried red chilli, crumbled

20 salted anchovy fillets, prepared (see page 346), 8 fillets kept whole, the rest chopped

2 tablespoons plain flour

1/2 nutmeg, freshly grated

200 g (7 oz) black olives, stoned

120 g (4.1/2 oz) Parmesan, freshly grated

Preheat the oven to 190° C/375° F/Gas 5.

Blanch the chard leaves for 3 minutes in boiling salted water. Drain, keeping the cooking liquid. Slice the chard stalks 1 cm (1/2 in) thick. Put the stalks with 500 ml (17 fl oz) of the blanching water in a separate saucepan. Add the vinegar, bay leaves, thyme branches (not the leaves) and black pepper; test for salt. Simmer for 8 minutes. Drain, keeping the cooking liquid.

Melt two-thirds of the butter in a heavy-bottomed saucepan and fry the onion until soft and beginning to go brown. Add the garlic, chard stalks, thyme leaves and chilli. Fry just to cook the garlic, then add the chopped anchovies. Combine the anchovies with the vegetables, then add the flour, stir and cook over a low heat for 6-8 minutes. Slowly add the chard cooking liquid, stirring to combine and thicken until you have a thick sauce, the consistency of double cream. (You may not need all the liquid.) Season with nutmeg, pepper and salt if necessary.

Grease a china or terracotta baking dish with a little of the remaining butter. Spread half of the anchovy sauce and chard stalks over the bottom, then carefully cover with the chard leaves. Place over half the olives. Drizzle over the remainder of the anchovy and stalk mixture. Put little bits of butter on top along with the remaining anchovies, the remainder of the olives and a few thyme leaves. Scatter over the Parmesan.

Bake in the preheated oven for 25 minutes. The top should be coloured, the olives slightly roasted.

Patate con finocchio e porcini
Potatoes with fennel and porcini

For 6

175 g (6 oz) dried porcini
4 tablespoons olive oil
4 garlic cloves, peeled and cut into slivers
8 medium fennel bulbs, trimmed and cut lengthways into 1 cm (1/2 in) slices
1.5 kg (3.1/4 lb) potatoes (Linska or Roseval), peeled and cut into 1 cm (1/2 in) slices
Maldon salt and freshly ground black pepper

Preheat the oven to 200° C/400° F/Gas 6.

In this recipe, it is essential that the potatoes, fennel and porcini are of the same thickness. As they are baked in one layer, a large shallow baking tray should be used.

Soak the porcini in about 175 ml (6 fl oz) hot water for half an hour, then drain carefully through a fine sieve, retaining the soaking water. Heat 1 tablespoon of the oil in a pan, then gently fry the porcini with a little of the garlic for a few minutes. The porcini slices should be slightly browned. Add about 3 tablespoons of the soaking liquid, and continue to cook until soft, and most of the liquid has evaporated.

In a very large saucepan heat the rest of the olive oil, then add the rest of the garlic slivers plus the fennel slices. Cook, stirring, for 5-10 minutes, or until the fennel is soft. Add the potatoes and stir thoroughly, then add the porcini and salt and pepper to taste. Stir together well, then put in one layer in the baking tray. Place in the preheated oven and cook for 30 minutes or until the potatoes are cooked.

Topinambur con parmigiano
Jerusalem artichokes and parmesan

For 6

2 kg (4.1/2 lb) Jerusalem artichokes
1/2 lemon
4 garlic cloves, peeled
3 tablespoons fresh thyme leaves
3 teaspoons Maldon salt
freshly ground black pepper
75 g (3 oz) unsalted butter
150 g (5 oz) Parmesan, grated
150 ml (5 fl oz) Chicken Stock (see page 142)
150 ml (5 fl oz) double cream

Preheat the oven to 200° C/400° F/Gas 6.

Peel the artichokes and slice lengthways into thick slices. Put the slices in cold water with the half lemon to prevent browning. Remove and dry.

Crush the garlic with the thyme to a fine paste. Mix the artichokes with the paste and season.

Butter a suitable baking dish, and place the artichokes in a couple of layers. Scatter with half the Parmesan. Pour over the stock and dot with the remaining butter. Cover with foil and bake for 20 minutes. Remove the foil, and turn the artichoke slices over. Scatter with the remaining Parmesan, add the cream, and bake for a further 10 minutes. Most of the liquid should have reduced, and the top will be crisp and brown.

Patate e acciughe al forno
Potato and anchovy gratin

For 6

1 kg (2.1/4 lb) Linska potatoes, or similar yellow waxy variety

2 tablespoons olive oil

50 g (2 oz) unsalted butter

6 garlic cloves, peeled and sliced

20 salted anchovy fillets, prepared (see page 346)

1 teaspoon finely chopped fresh rosemary

2 dried red chillies, crumbled

100 g (4 oz) Parmesan, freshly grated

300 ml (10 fl oz) double cream

Maldon salt and freshly ground black pepper

3 tablespoons chopped flat-leaf parsley

Preheat the oven to 190° C/375° F/Gas 5. Peel the potatoes and cut lengthways into 5 mm (1/4 in) thick slices. Put into cold water to soak off the starch for 5 minutes.

Heat the oil and butter in a small saucepan. Add the garlic and gently fry for 2 minutes then add the anchovy fillets. Break up and melt the anchovies into a sauce. Add the rosemary and chilli. Stir to combine, then remove the pan from the heat.

Drain the potatoes, spread out on a cloth and pat dry. Place in a large bowl and add the anchovy sauce, three-quarters of the Parmesan and the cream. Season and toss together. Put in a baking tray, cover with foil and bake in the preheated oven for 25 minutes. Remove the foil, gently turn the potatoes over, then add the parsley. Test for seasoning, then scatter over the remaining Parmesan. Continue to bake for a further 15 minutes. The potatoes should be lightly browned and crisp.

Veget
in pac

ables

ella

7

Carciofi in padella   Frittedda   Piselli, fave e lenticch
semi di finocchio   Cicoria brasate   Porri e carciofi bra

t'olio   Cime di rapa brasate   Cavolo nero brasate con
Peperoni in padella   Zucchini, prosciutto e menta

Carciofi in padella
Artichokes braised with white wine

For 6

12 small globe artichokes, with stalks, prepared (see page 172)

1 lemon, halved

olive oil

1 bunch fresh thyme, leaves picked from the stalks

4 garlic cloves, peeled and thinly sliced

Maldon salt and freshly ground black pepper

150 ml (5 fl oz) dry white wine

Prepare the artichokes, then rub with a lemon half to prevent discolouring.

In a large heavy saucepan heat 2 tablespoons of the olive oil over a medium heat. Fry the artichokes until they begin to colour, then add the thyme and garlic. Season generously with salt and pepper. Stir occasionally.

When the garlic begins to colour, add the white wine, the juice from the remaining lemon half, and enough olive oil, about 150 ml (5 fl oz), to cover. Put the lid on, and simmer gently for about 30 minutes, or until the artichokes are tender.

Frittedda
Braised broad beans, peas and artichokes

For 6

6 small young artichokes, prepared (see page 172), cut into quarters
500 g (18 oz) fresh peas, shelled weight (use only young fresh peas)
300 g (10 oz) broad beans, shelled weight (use only young fresh beans)
2 red onions, peeled and finely sliced
5 tablespoons extra virgin olive oil
2 tablespoons roughly chopped fresh flat-leaf parsley
3 tablespoons roughly chopped fresh mint leaves
Maldon salt and freshly ground black pepper
juice of 2 lemons

In a large heavy saucepan, gently fry the onion in 2 tablespoons of the oil until golden. Add the artichoke quarters and over a medium heat stir and cook until al dente, about 15 minutes. Add the peas and broad beans and enough water to moisten, about 150 ml (5 fl oz). Cook until the peas and beans are tender, a further 5-10 minutes.

Stir in the parsley and mint, and season with salt, pepper, lemon juice and the remainder of the extra virgin olive oil.

Serve at room temperature.

Piselli, fave e lenticchie sott'olio

For 6

1.5 kg (3.1/4 lb) each of peas and broad beans in their pods
175 g (6 oz) Puy or Castelluccio lentils, washed
2 garlic cloves, peeled
extra virgin olive oil
1 lemon, halved
Maldon salt and freshly ground black pepper
1 large bunch fresh mint, chopped

Shell the peas and broad beans separately, keeping aside any that are particularly large as they take longer to cook.

Cover the lentils with cold water, add the garlic, and bring to the boil. Simmer gently for about 20 minutes until al dente or nutty in texture. Drain, discard the garlic, and toss the lentils in enough olive oil to coat them well, plus a squeeze of lemon juice. Season with salt and pepper.

Blanch the peas first (large, then small) in plenty of salted water for about 1 minute or according to size (the salt keeps the peas green). Drain well, toss while hot with extra virgin olive oil, and season.

Blanch the broad beans in boiling water (*no* salt), and cook for about 2-3 minutes, or longer for the larger ones. Drain well, toss while hot with oil, and season.

Mix the lentils, peas and broad beans together in a bowl, adding more olive oil if necessary. Add the mint and season once again. Serve warm or at room temperature.

Cime di rapa brasate
Braised cime di rapa

For 6

2 kg (4.1/2 lb) cime di rapa
Maldon salt and freshly ground black pepper
extra virgin olive oil
4 garlic cloves, peeled and finely sliced
2 small dried red chillies, crumbled

Pick through the cime de rapa and discard any really large, tough outer leaves. Cut off and discard the tough stalks. Keep the sprouting heads and young leaves. Wash the heads and leaves carefully. Blanch for 5 minutes in boiling, salted water. Drain and lay out to dry.

In a heavy-bottomed pan heat 3 tablespoons of olive oil, and add the garlic slices and dried chilli. As the garlic is about to turn in colour, add the blanched cime de rapa and toss for a minute. Season with salt and pepper and serve drizzled with extra virgin olive oil.

Cavolo nero brasate con semi di finocchio
Braised cavolo nero with fennel seeds

For 6

2 kg (4.1/2 lb) cavolo nero
Maldon salt and freshly ground black pepper
extra virgin olive oil
4 garlic cloves, peeled and thinly sliced
20 fennel seeds, crushed

To prepare the cavolo nero, hold the stalk firmly in one hand and strip away the leaves from the stems with the other. Briefly blanch the cavolo leaves in plenty of boiling salted water until they are marginally undercooked, about 5 minutes. They should be a brilliant green colour. Drain well and lay out to dry.

Heat enough oil to cover the base of a large saucepan. Add the garlic and gently fry. When it begins to colour, add the crushed fennel seeds and fry for a minute more before adding the cavolo nero. Stir-fry for 5 minutes to allow the cavolo to absorb the flavours. Season well and serve.

Cicoria brasate
Braised bitter cicoria

For 6 In Italian markets you can also find puntarelle, part of the same family as cicoria. It is sold when it is sprouting like broccoli and can be cooked in a similar way or eaten as a salad served with warm anchovy sauce (see page 308).

1.75 kg (4 lb) cicoria leaves
Maldon salt and freshly ground black pepper
3 tablespoons extra virgin olive oil
3 garlic cloves, peeled and thinly sliced
2 small dried red chillies (optional)

To prepare the cicoria, remove the tough outer leaves and then cut the cicoria hearts off at the root. Heat a large pot of boiling salted water, and blanch the cicoria until tender, about 5 minutes. Drain well and lay out to dry.

In a separate pan heat the olive oil and fry the garlic and chilli (if using) lightly. Add the cicoria, salt and pepper, and cook for about 5-10 minutes, stirring.

You can serve this cold, as part of an antipasto, or mixed with some cooked borlotti beans.

Porri e carciofi brasate
Braised leeks and artichokes

For 6

1.5 kg (3.1/4 lb) leeks
6 small or 3 large artichokes
1 lemon, halved
2 tablespoons olive oil
3 garlic cloves, peeled and finely sliced
2 tablespoons chopped fresh mint leaves
Maldon salt and freshly ground black pepper
120 ml (4 fl oz) white wine
2-3 tablespoons roughly chopped fresh flat-leaf parsley

Peel the outer leaves from the leeks, and trim the roots and the larger tough green parts. Wash thoroughly and shake dry. Cut the leeks in diagonal dice about 1 cm (1/2 in) thick. Prepare the artichokes as on page 172, until you are left with the pale tender heart. Peel the fibre from the stalks of smaller artichokes; discard the stalks of larger artichokes, as they are too tough. Cut each artichoke heart in eighths and scrape away any choke or prickly violet leaves. Place in a bowl of water with the lemon halves as you cut, then drain and dry.

Heat the oil in a large heavy saucepan with a lid. When hot add the artichoke slices and cook quickly until lightly coloured, then add the leeks. Stir-fry together for 5 minutes then add the garlic, mint, salt and pepper. When the garlic has softened, add the wine and stir to scrape up any artichoke and leek stuck on the bottom. Cover with a lid and cook until the wine has evaporated, about 10-15 minutes. Add the parsley, taste for seasoning, and serve.

Peperoni in padella
Peppers in olive oil

For 6

8 large ripe dark red peppers
4 tablespoons olive oil
Maldon salt and freshly ground black pepper
3 tablespoons herb wine vinegar (Volpaia 'Erbe')

Wash and dry the peppers, then cut in half lengthways and then in half again and again. Using a small paring knife, remove any white membrane on the inside of the peppers, plus the seeds.

Use a large frying pan or low-sided large saucepan with a lid. Heat half the olive oil and place some of the pepper pieces in one layer. Fry over a medium to high heat with the lid on, turning the pieces over as they begin to colour and become soft. Remove with a slotted spoon and keep warm. Repeat with a second layer of peppers, and continue until you have cooked them all. You may have to use extra oil if you fry in more than two batches. Drain off excess oil.

Return all the peppers to the pan, reheat together, and season with salt, pepper and vinegar.

Zucchini, Prosciutto e Menta

For 6

900 g (2 lb) zucchini
3 garlic cloves, peeled
3-4 tablespoons olive oil
Maldon salt and freshly ground black pepper
1 large bunch mint, leaves removed from the stalks, coarsely chopped
9 slices prosciutto, cut into wide strips
extra virgin olive oil

Trim the ends of the zucchini, cut lengthways into quarters and then again into 4 cm (1.1/2 in) pieces, slicing diagonally with your knife. If the garlic cloves are small, leave whole; if not, cut in half lengthways.

In a thick-bottomed frying pan with a lid, heat the olive oil over a moderate flame. Add the garlic, the zucchini, salt and pepper, and toss. Cook the zucchini until tender but crisp and slightly brown, about 15 minutes.

Remove from the heat, place all the mint leaves evenly over the zucchini, followed by the prosciutto. Immediately cover with the tight-fitting lid, and let sit until ready to serve.

Drizzle with extra virgin olive oil, season again, and toss gently. Serve at room temperature.

Fish
Shel

lfish

8

Zuppa di pesce
Fish soup

For 8

3 small lobsters, each about 450 g (1 lb) in weight, halved

6 x 150 g (5 oz) fillets of sea bream or red mullet, scaled

500 g (18 oz) mussels or clams, scrubbed

12 live prawns or langoustines

4 tablespoons olive oil

2 small red onions, peeled and finely chopped

3 garlic cloves, peeled and chopped

1-2 tablespoons dried oregano

3 small dried red chillies, crumbled

1.5 kg (3.1/4 lb) ripe plum or other tomatoes, skinned, seeded and roughly chopped

250 ml (8 fl oz) white wine

12 medium Linska or other yellow waxy potatoes, scrubbed and cut in to 5 cm (2 in)
    pieces

Maldon salt and freshly ground black pepper

4 tablespoons chopped fresh flat-leaf parsley

8 crostini (see page 290)

extra virgin olive oil

Heat the olive oil in a very large heavy saucepan big enough to hold all the fish, or two medium to large pans.

Add the onion and fry gently until soft and turning gold, then add the garlic, oregano and chilli, and cook for 2 minutes. Add the tomato and continue to cook gently.

When the tomato begins to break up, add the wine, bring to the boil, then add the potato. Cook the potato for 5 minutes, then add the lobsters. Put the lid on and simmer gently for 3-4 minutes, then add the bream or mullet fillets and carry on simmering for a further 5 minutes.

Add the mussels or clams and the prawns. Season with salt and pepper, replace the lid, and simmer for a further 5-6 minutes. The mussels or clams should have opened (discard any that remain closed), and the fish should be perfectly cooked. Add the chopped parsley to the liquor.

Serve with crostini drizzled with extra virgin olive oil.

Gamberetti fritti
Deep-fried shrimps

For 6 Poole prawns are in season from June to September in a warm summer, and are caught in pots that the Dorset fishermen make specially for the purpose. The prawns are brown, about 3 cm (1.1/2 in) long excluding the whiskers, and are sold live.

1.5 kg (3.1/4 lb) live Poole prawns or similar brown shrimps
sunflower oil for deep-frying
Maldon salt and freshly ground black pepper
Chilli sauce
4 medium to large fresh red chillies, seeded and finely chopped
200 ml (7 fl oz) extra virgin olive oil
juice of 1 lemon
Herb salad
300 g (10 oz) altogether of mixed herb leaves (dill, red and green basil, mint, rocket)
3 tablespoons of extra virgin olive oil
2 tablespoons of lemon juice

For the chilli sauce, mix the ingredients together and season with salt and pepper.

To prepare the prawns – which are eaten whole – cut off the unicorn spike on the head of each, using scissors.

Heat the oil to 180° C/350° F. Deep-fry the prawns in batches that will fit into your fryer, just for 1 minute. They will turn bright pink as they cook. Drain well on kitchen paper, then season generously with salt and pepper.

Serve the prawns hot with the chilli sauce and dressed herb salad.

Cozze al forno con zucchini, capperi e peperoni
Baked mussels with zucchini, capers and peppers

For 6

3 kg (6.1/2 lb) mussels, thoroughly cleaned

3 tablespoons olive oil

1 medium red onion, peeled and finely sliced

4 garlic cloves, peeled and finely sliced

2 small dried red chillies, crumbled

150 ml (5 fl oz) dry white wine

1 kg (2.1/4 lb) ripe plum tomatoes, skinned, seeded and chopped, or 1 x 800 g
(1.3/4 lb) tin peeled plum tomatoes, drained of their juices

Maldon salt and freshly ground black pepper

3 small zucchini, trimmed

3 yellow peppers

3 tablespoons salted capers, prepared (see page 346), and then soaked in 2
tablespoons red wine vinegar

6 tablespoons chopped fresh flat-leaf parsley

extra virgin olive oil

2 lemons

In a large saucepan heat the olive oil and gently fry the onion until soft and beginning to colour. Add the garlic, cook for a minute, then add the dried red chilli, half the white wine and the tomatoes. Cook together for half an hour – the sauce should have begun to thicken. Season generously.

Cut the zucchini in half lengthways and then into 2 mm (1/8 in) slices. In a separate pan of boiling salted water, blanch the zucchini for just 1 minute. Drain immediately.

Grill the peppers on all sides until the skin is black, then cool in a plastic bag. When cool, remove the skins, seeds and any thick white fibres from the insides. Cut the flesh into 1 cm (1/2 in) cubes.

Use a large open casserole, high-sided roasting tin or a stainless-steel saucepan that will go in your oven. Spoon the tomato sauce on to the bottom of the pan. Add the capers, cover with the mussels, the zucchini and peppers. Pour over the remaining white wine, shake over half the parsley, and drizzle with a little extra virgin olive oil. Place in the hot oven and bake for 10 minutes or until all the mussels have opened, discarding any that remain closed.

Serve in large flat soup bowls with the remainder of the parsley, more extra virgin olive oil and a slice of lemon.

Aragosta al forno
Wood-roasted lobster

For 6

6 live lobsters, weighing about 450 g (1 lb) each
Maldon salt and freshly ground black pepper
2 dried red chillies, crumbled
1 tablespoon dried oregano
3 lemons
4 tablespoons extra virgin olive oil
3 large red fresh chillies, seeded and chopped
4 tablespoons chopped flat-leaf parsley
6 lemon wedges

Preheat the oven to 240° C/475° F/Gas 9.

Place the live lobsters face down on a board. Use a large sharp pointed knife to split them down the centre. Remove the little sac found near the head. Crack the claws so that you can easily pick the flesh out when the lobster is cooked.

Season the flesh of the lobsters with salt, pepper and dried chilli, sprinkle with oregano and squeeze over the juice of 2 lemons. Place on baking trays and roast in the preheated very hot oven for 15 minutes. The shell of the lobster should turn red and the flesh should gently brown.

Mix the oil with the chopped fresh chilli and parsley, then add a tablespoon of lemon juice. Drizzle this sauce over each lobster. Serve with lemon wedges.

Insalata di polpa di granchio
Crab salad

For 6 Live crabs should be kept in the fridge so they are cold and go to sleep.

3 live crabs, about 1-1.4 kg (2-3 lb) each in weight
Maldon salt and freshly ground black pepper
juice of 2 lemons
6 tablespoons extra virgin olive oil
4 medium fresh chillies, seeded and chopped
1 small bunch green fennel herb, roughly chopped
6 lemon wedges
a handful of rocket leaves
6 sourdough bruschetta (see page 290)

Put each crab in its own large saucepan of cold water. Add 50 g (2 oz) of salt to each pan, cover, and very slowly bring the water to the boil. The crabs are cooked when the water reaches boiling point. Remove the crabs from the pans, drain and leave to cool.

Break each crab open by pulling away the upper body shell. Scrape out the brown meat and put into a bowl. Break the claws and legs from the body, crack and pick out the white meat, keeping the pieces as large as possible. Place in a separate bowl.

Mix two-thirds of the lemon juice with the oil and chilli, then season. Add to the bowl of white meat. Season the brown meat with salt, pepper and the remaining lemon juice only.

Cover half of each bruschetta generously with brown crab meat and half with white meat. Sprinkle over the fennel, and serve with a lemon wedge and rocket leaves.

Baccalà
Salt cod

For 6 It is best to buy a whole cod – of about 2.25-2.75 kg (5-6 lb), say – and to take it home and fillet it yourself. It is important that the salting process is started the moment you have finished filleting in order to prevent deterioration of the cut side of the fish. Maldon salt is not suitable for this recipe.

1 kg (2.1/4 lb) very fresh fillet of cod with skin intact
1 kg (2.1/4 lb) natural coarse sea salt

Use a flat board, and arrange this in a tray, with a saucer placed under one end to make it slant at an angle.

Cover the board with a layer of salt about 1 cm (1/2 in) deep. Place the fish, skin side down, on top of the salt. Cover the other side of the fish with 1 cm (1/2 in) of salt. Put in the fridge for 24 hours minimum – 5 days maximum.

Remove the salt by rinsing the fish under a running cold tap for 5 minutes. Then place in a bath of water for 6 hours, changing the water as frequently as possible.

Inzimino di baccalà
Salt cod with chickpeas

For 6

600 g (1 lb, 6 oz) salt cod (see page 212), cut into 5 cm (2 in) pieces

175 g (6 oz) dried chickpeas, soaked overnight

1 large potato, peeled

5 large garlic cloves, peeled, and 3 sliced finely

1 sprig each of fresh thyme, bay and sage

3 tablespoons olive oil

2 small dried red chillies, crumbled

1 x 800 g (1.3/4 lb) peeled plum tomatoes, drained of their juices

Maldon salt and freshly ground black pepper

900 g (2 lb) Swiss chard, large stems removed, blanched and roughly chopped

250 ml (8 fl oz) white wine

3 tablespoons chopped fresh flat-leaf parsley

Put the chickpeas into a saucepan with the potato, 2 whole garlic cloves and the herbs. Cover with cold water, bring to the boil and skim the surface. Turn the heat down and simmer for 1-1.1/2 hours. Keep the chickpeas in their cooking liquid until you use them.

Heat 2 tablespoons of oil in a thick-bottomed pan. Add half the sliced garlic, cook to soften a little, then add half the chilli and the tomatoes. Cook for 30 minutes. Season.

Heat the remaining oil in a thick-bottomed pan. Add the rest of the garlic and fry briefly. Place the cod on the garlic, brown on both sides then add the wine. Reduce the heat and simmer for a few minutes until the cod is cooked. Season with pepper and chilli. Add the skinned chickpeas (see page 346) to the tomato sauce. Gently heat for 2-3 minutes then add the chard and the cod, with the pan juices. Sprinkle with the parsley.

Insalata di baccalà
Salt cod salad

For 6

1.5 kg (3.1/4 lb) baccalà (salt cod, see page 212)

1 small bunch parsley, leaves picked from the stalks, roughly chopped (keep the
    stalks for the stock)

Maldon salt and freshly ground black pepper

1 garlic clove, peeled and crushed with a little salt

juice of 3 lemons

150 ml (5 fl oz) extra virgin olive oil

6 fresh red chillies, seeded and chopped

200 g (7 oz) rocket leaves, washed and dried

225 g (8 oz) black Niçoise olives, stoned

6 bruschetta (see page 290)

Stock

4 fresh bay leaves

1 fennel bulb, cut into 4, including the green parts, or a handful of fresh fennel leaves

1/2 whole head garlic

2 carrots, peeled

1 small red onion, peeled

1/2 head celery

2 tablespoons black peppercorns

Soak the salt cod in fresh water, changing the water as many times as possible, for at least 48 hours. Drain thoroughly.

Put the cod in a large pot with the stock ingredients and the stalks of the parsley. Cover with cold water, bring to the boil, and very gently simmer until the cod is tender and flakes easily, about 15-20 minutes. Drain well and leave to cool.

When cool enough to handle, pull the cod apart into flakes. Put in a bowl and season with black pepper to taste, the salt-crushed garlic and a little of the lemon juice and olive oil. Turn the cod over once or twice in the bowl to season each flake, then add the chopped parsley leaves and the chilli.

Put the rocket leaves in a large serving bowl and toss with the remaining olive oil and lemon juice, then add the seasoned salt cod. Scatter over the olives. Turn gently together to combine, and serve with bruschetta.

Strati di sardine
Layered sardine sandwich

For 6 The following quantity of sardines will give you six fillets per portion; you might want to do eight fillets per person for a main course.

18 large very fresh sardines

olive oil

150 g (5 oz) breadcrumbs

grated zest of 2 lemons

200 g (7 oz) pine nuts

3 small dried red chillies, crumbled

1 bunch fresh flat-leaf parsley, leaves picked from their stalks, finely chopped

Maldon salt and freshly ground black pepper

3 lemons, thickly sliced

Preheat the oven to 200° C/400° F/Gas 6.

First scale the sardines, then slit the stomach with your knife and remove the guts. Cut the head off, following the angle of the gills. Make an incision with your knife, cutting in towards the backbone, and along the spine of the fish, carefully cutting the fillet away from the bone. Repeat on the other side. Sardines have a lot of very fine bones which are attached to the backbone. Trim any large bones that remain on the fillets.

Brush a baking tray with olive oil and lay three of the fillets skin side down next to each other. Sprinkle with some of the breadcrumbs, lemon zest, pine nuts, dried chilli, parsley, salt and pepper. Then lay another three fillets directly over the top, skin side up. Sprinkle with more breadcrumbs, lemon zest, dried chilli, parsley, pine nuts, salt and pepper. This is one portion. Repeat this process until you have six sandwiches.

Drizzle the sandwiches lightly with olive oil and bake in the preheated oven for about 6-8 minutes. Serve with lemon slices.

Trigliette al vino bianco, prezzemolo e aglio
Red mullet with white wine, parsley and garlic

For 6

12 small red mullet, scaled and cleaned

6 tablespoons olive oil

1 small bunch fresh flat-leaf parsley, finely chopped

3 garlic cloves, peeled and finely chopped

3/4 bottle white wine

6 pugliese bruschetta (see page 290)

Preheat the oven to 230° C/450° F/Gas 8.

In a small frying pan heat the olive oil, and cook the parsley and the garlic over low heat until soft.

Arrange the mullet in a roasting tray, then pour in the wine along with the oil, parsley and garlic. Place over moderate heat and bring just to the boil, then put in the preheated oven for 10 minutes.

Put a piece of bruschetta and 2 red mullet on each plate, and serve immediately.

Calamari ripiene con peperoncino al forno
Wood-roasted squid stuffed with chilli

For 6 as a starter

6 squid, the size of an adult hand, about 20 cm (8 in)
juice of 2 lemons and 3 whole lemons, halved
120 ml (4 fl oz) extra virgin olive oil
5 large fresh red chillies, seeded and chopped
Maldon salt and freshly ground black pepper
1 garlic clove, peeled and finely chopped
3 tablespoons chopped fresh flat-leaf parsley
1 tablespoon dried oregano
200 g (7 oz) rocket leaves, washed and dried

Preheat the oven to 230° C/450° F/Gas 8.

Clean the squid by pulling the tentacles and head away from the body. Turn the body sac inside out and scrape away the guts remaining. Turn the body sac right side out again. Cut the head and beak off the tentacles, and discard.

Mix 2 tablespoons of the lemon juice with 4 tablespoons of the olive oil, then add half the chilli, some salt and pepper and the garlic. Stir in 1 tablespoon of the chopped parsley. Put some of this mixture inside each squid, dividing it equally. Mix the rest of the chilli with 3 tablespoons of the remaining olive oil, and season.

Heat a large oven dish, and brush with the rest of the olive oil. Sprinkle the oregano and some salt and pepper over each squid, then place in the hot oil. Turn over and place in the oven. Roast for 5-6 minutes; they should be slightly brown. Serve with the chilli sauce, the remaining parsley, rocket leaves and lemon halves.

Spiedini di coda di rospo e cappesante
Spiedini of monkfish and scallops

For 6

12 medium fresh scallops, preferably bought live in the shell
500 g (18 oz) monkfish tail, boned and skinned
6 x 15 cm (6 in) rosemary branches
Maldon salt and freshly ground black pepper
Anchovy and Rosemary Sauce (see page 308)
2 lemons, cut into wedges

For each spiedino you need 2 scallops and 2 cubes of monkfish. Pull the leaves off the rosemary stalks, leaving just the tufts at the end. Sharpen the other end into a point.

To prepare the scallops, place them, flat shell side down, on a board. Insert a sharp knife close to the hinge and prise open. Remove the whole scallop from the bottom shell by gently cutting, keeping the blade flat; use a gentle sawing motion. The whole scallop will now be cupped in the top curved half of the shell. Use a tablespoon and carefully scoop out the scallop; trim off the membrane. Wash, then pat dry.

Cut the monkfish into cubes roughly the same size as the scallops. Thread a scallop on first, making sure the rosemary stick goes through the white muscle part and the coral. Next thread on a piece of monkfish, then the other scallop, and finally the other piece of monkfish.

Heat a char-grill or griddle pan. When very hot, place the spiedini on and grill. Season with salt and pepper whilst grilling. Turn over after 3 minutes or when the spiedini no longer stick but have sealed and are brown. Grill for a further few minutes.

Serve the spiedini with Anchovy and Rosemary Sauce, along with wedges of lemon.

Salmone selvatico fiammeggiato
Seared wild salmon

For 6

1 x 3.6 kg (8 lb) wild salmon
Maldon salt and freshly ground black pepper
3 lemons

Place the salmon on its side on a board. With a very sharp filleting knife, slice the head off behind the gills. You will expose the main bone. Place one hand on the top side of the salmon to keep it in place and with your other hand cut along the top of the bone, keeping the blade of your knife angled towards the bone, using the finger and thumb of your other hand to lift the side of salmon away as you cut. You will be cutting through the small fillet bones as you go. Turn the salmon over and repeat the process. You will need to pinbone your two fillets with tweezers. Trim the belly sides of the fillets free of fat.

To portion your pieces of salmon, place one side skin-side down on your board. You are aiming to get six portions altogether, three from each fillet. Divide the side equally into three by eye, and cut into the salmon at about a 45 degree angle, cutting straight through the skin at the bottom.

Season your pieces of salmon with salt and pepper, and grill skin-side down first on a preheated very hot grill pan or char-grill for about 1 minute until just seared. Turn over and sear the flesh side. Serve with wedges of lemon.

Salmone selvatico al sale
Wild salmon baked whole in sea salt

For 8

1 x 3.6 kg (8 lb) whole wild salmon, scaled and cleaned
Maldon salt and freshly ground black pepper
1 large bunch fresh fennel leaves and stalks, washed
5-6 kg (11-13 lb) natural coarse sea salt

Preheat the oven to 220° C/425° F/Gas 7.

Season the salmon well with pepper and salt on the inside only. Fill the gut cavity with the fresh fennel leaves and stalks (there is no need to chop them up).

Cover the bottom of a large roasting tray with a layer of salt 1 cm (1/2 in) deep. Place the salmon on the salt. Pile the salt over the fish so that it is completely covered by at least 1 cm (1/2 in) all over. Do not worry if the head and tail protrude.

Sprinkle a few tablespoons of water over the surface of the salt.

Place the salmon in the hot oven and bake for about 20 minutes. To test if the fish is cooked, pierce the salt with a skewer and into the fish at a place where the fish is thickest. If it is warm, the salmon is cooked. Remove from the oven, and allow to cool to a temperature you can handle.

Break off the salt crust from the top of the fish; the skin should have stuck to the salt and come away as you do this. Gently lift the whole fish out of the roasting tray. Peel away any skin and salt stuck to the underside and place the fish on a board.

Pull the fillets off the bones. Serve at room temperature with Basil Mayonnaise or Anchovy and Caper Mayonnaise, or Salsa Verde (see pages 310 and 311).

Rombo con rosmarino al sale
Whole turbot with rosemary baked in sea salt

For 6 Buy a fresh turbot that is not thick with roe and still has sea slime on its skin. Have the fishmonger remove only the gut.

1 turbot with head and tail intact, about 2.75-3.25 kg (6-7 lb)
3.4 kg (7.1/2 lb) natural coarse sea salt
1 bunch fresh rosemary
freshly ground black pepper
balsamic vinegar (aged and thick)
extra virgin olive oil
3 lemons

Preheat the oven to 220° C/425° F/Gas 7.

Use a large baking tray that will snugly hold the turbot. Cover the bottom with a layer of salt, and place the turbot on the salt. Push the rosemary into the cavity and completely cover the fish with the remainder of the salt, about 1.5 cm (3/4 in) thick. Do not worry if the head and tail protrude. Sprinkle the surface of the salt very lightly with a little water – use a few tablespoons.

Place in the preheated oven and bake for 25-35 minutes. After 20 minutes test by inserting a skewer into the centre of the fish; if it is warm, the turbot is cooked.

Allow to cool for 5 minutes, then crack open the salt crust. Carefully remove as much of the salt as possible. You will find the thick skin of the turbot will stick to the salt.

Serve at room temperature, with coarsely ground black pepper, a few dribbles of balsamic vinegar, extra virgin olive oil and a half lemon.

Trancio di rombo al forno con capperi
Wood-roasted turbot tranche with capers

For 6

6 slices turbot on the bone, about 225-300 g (8-10 oz) each
2 tablespoons olive oil
Maldon salt and freshly ground black pepper
juice of 3 lemons
6 tablespoons chopped green celery leaves (the younger leaves are best)
6 tablespoons chopped fresh flat-leaf parsley
12 tablespoons salted capers, prepared (see page 346)
1 lemon, sliced

Preheat the oven to 230° C/450° F/Gas 8.

Brush the fish lightly with olive oil, and season with salt and pepper. Place in one layer on a flat baking tray. Bake in the preheated oven for 15-20 minutes, according to the size of the slices.

Remove from the oven and put the fish on serving plates. Add the lemon juice, celery leaves, half the parsley and the capers to the baking tray, and heat for about a minute over a high flame to combine the fish juices with the lemon juice.

Serve, pouring the capers and the juices over the turbot. Sprinkle the remainder of the parsley on top, and serve with a slice of lemon.

Branzino ripieno d'erbe
Sea bass slashed and stuffed with herbs

For 6

1 sea bass, about 3.2-3.6 kg (7-8 lb) in weight, scaled and cleaned, or 6 x 175-200 g
   (6-7 oz) individual sea bass fillets
Maldon salt and freshly ground black pepper
2 tablespoons each of fresh marjoram, fresh basil or mint, and fresh green fennel or
   dill, roughly chopped
3 lemons
100 ml (3.1/2 fl oz) extra virgin olive oil

Preheat the grill or griddle. It must be very hot and clean.

Make 1 cm (1/2 in) deep slashes across the width of the whole sea bass at 6 cm
(2.1/2 in) intervals. Slash the skin side of the fillets in the same way. Season the fish
with salt and pepper. Mix the herbs together and then push as much of this mixture
into the slashes as you can.

Place the whole fish on the grill and do not turn over until it is completely sealed.
Turn over when the fish comes away easily. When sealed on both sides, reduce the
heat and continue grilling until the fish is cooked. Alternatively, grill the fillets, skin
side down first, on the grill.

Mix the juice of 1 of the lemons with the olive oil, and pour over the grilled fish, then
scatter any remaining herbs over. Serve with lemon wedges.

Sogliola al forno con origano e alloro
Roasted dover sole with oregano and bay

For 6

6 whole Dover sole, weighing about 350-400 g (12-14 oz) each, scaled and cleaned
extra virgin olive oil
6 lemons
24 dried bay leaves
4 tablespoons dried wild oregano
Maldon salt and coarsely ground black pepper

Preheat the oven to 230° C/450° F/Gas 8.

Brush your flat oven trays with olive oil. Slice 2 of the lemons into fine discs 1 mm (1/16 in) thick. Scatter half the bay leaves, a few of the lemon slices and some oregano on the bottom of the trays. Place the soles on top, season generously with salt and pepper, then scatter the remaining dried oregano, bay leaves and lemon slices on top of the fish to cover them. Drizzle generously with olive oil and bake in the preheated oven for 15-20 minutes. Test using the point of a sharp knife down the centre of the thickest part of the sole; if cooked, the flesh should just be coming away from the bone.

When cooked, remove the sole from the baking trays, and place on serving plates. Place the baking tray with its remaining herbs and fish juices over a medium heat and deglaze with the juice from 3 of the remaining lemons. Serve each sole with some of this sauce from the pan, the herb leaves and lemon wedges.

Tonno marinato e fiammeggiato
Seared marinated tuna

For 6 Mediterranean bluefin tuna is in season between mid June and mid August.

6 slices fresh bluefin tuna about 1.5 cm (3/4 in) thick, and about 200-225 g (7-8 oz)
 each in weight
3 garlic cloves, peeled and finely chopped
1 bunch fresh green fennel herb
1 teaspoon fennel seeds, ground in a mortar
2 small dried red chillies, crumbled
Maldon salt and freshly ground black pepper
200 ml (7 fl oz) white wine
100 ml (3.1/2 fl oz) olive oil
4 lemons

Place the tuna steaks on a board. Rub half the garlic into the fish, along with half the chopped fennel, fennel seeds, chilli and salt and pepper. Turn over and do the same on the other side.

Place the steaks side by side in a large flat container, and pour in the white wine, olive oil and the juice of 1 lemon. Cover and leave to marinate in a cool place for at least 1 hour.

Preheat the barbecue grill or griddle to very hot, and sear the tuna for only 1 minute on each side.

Serve hot with a wedge of lemon, and a sauce – Fresh Red Chilli and Fennel Sauce or Green Chilli and Lemon Peel Sauce (see pages 306 and 305).

Lombo di tonno al forno con coriandolo
Baked whole loin of tuna with coriander

For 8

3 kg (6.1/2 lb) loin of tuna in the piece, skin removed

4 garlic cloves, peeled and cut into slivers

3 tablespoons coriander seeds, lightly crushed

Maldon salt and freshly ground black pepper

1 bunch fresh mint, leaves picked from the stalks, roughly chopped

3 tablespoons extra virgin olive oil

1/2 bottle white wine

4 tablespoons salted capers, prepared (see page 346)

Tomato Sauce

1.5 kg (3.1/4 lb) ripe plum tomatoes, skinned, seeded and roughly chopped

3 tablespoons olive oil

4 garlic cloves, peeled and finely chopped

2-3 dried red chillies, crumbled

1 x 7.5 cm (3 in) cinnamon stick

1 teaspoon dried oregano

1 bunch fresh mint, leaves picked from the stalks, roughly chopped

2 large fresh red chillies, seeded and chopped

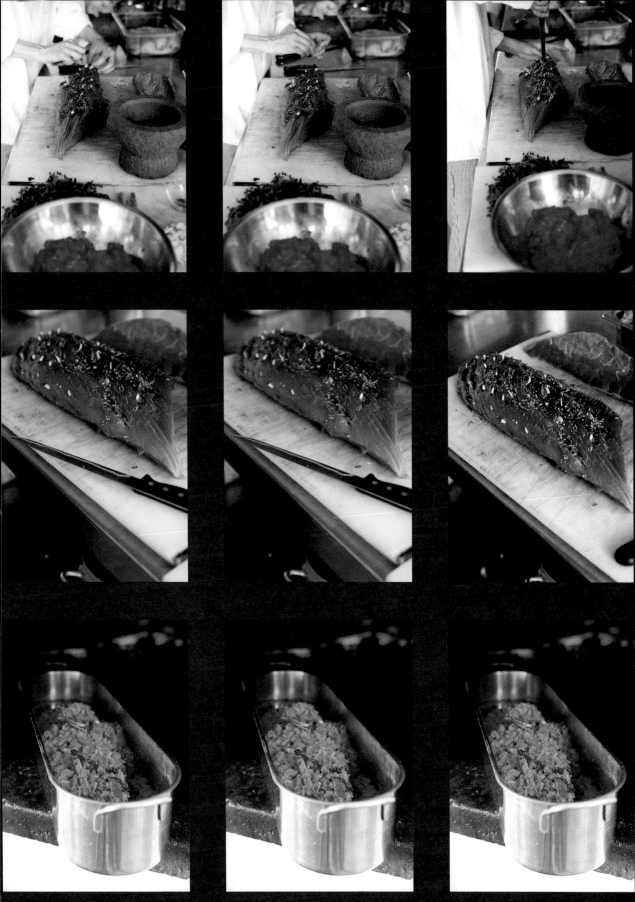

Trim the tuna loin of any sinew and very dark flesh, and skin it. To stud the loin, using a small sharp kitchen knife, make horizontal slits along the complete surface of the tuna, about 5 cm (2 in) apart, and 2 cm (3/4 in) deep. The flesh of a tuna has a natural flakiness; make sure you follow that when making the incisions. Into each slit push a sliver of garlic, a little coriander, some salt and pepper, and finally a little mint. This will take time as you must split and stuff all sides of the loin.

Preheat the oven to 220° C/425° F/Gas 7.

To make the tomato sauce, heat the olive oil in a large thick-bottomed pan. Add the garlic, dried chilli, the whole cinnamon stick, oregano and remaining coriander and fry together until the garlic begins to turn golden in colour. Then add the mint followed by the tomatoes and fresh chilli. Stir and cook together over the high heat for 10-15 minutes. The flavours should blend and the tomatoes should reduce a little. Season with salt and pepper.

Take a casserole or heavy roasting pan with a thick bottom, and heat the oil in it until very hot. Place the tuna in the pan and seal and brown on all sides. Remove the loin from the pan and pour off excess oil. Pour the wine into the pan to deglaze it, and allow to reduce a little, stirring and scraping. Return the tuna loin to the pan, and pour over the tomato sauce. This may not completely cover the loin; spoon some of the liquid over the top. Half cover the casserole, and put in the preheated oven to bake for up to 20 minutes or until cooked (rare tuna is delicious).

Place the loin on a large carving board and slice into thick slices. Serve with the tomato sauce, and sprinkled with the remaining chopped mint and the capers.

Pork C

Duck C

hicken

ame

9

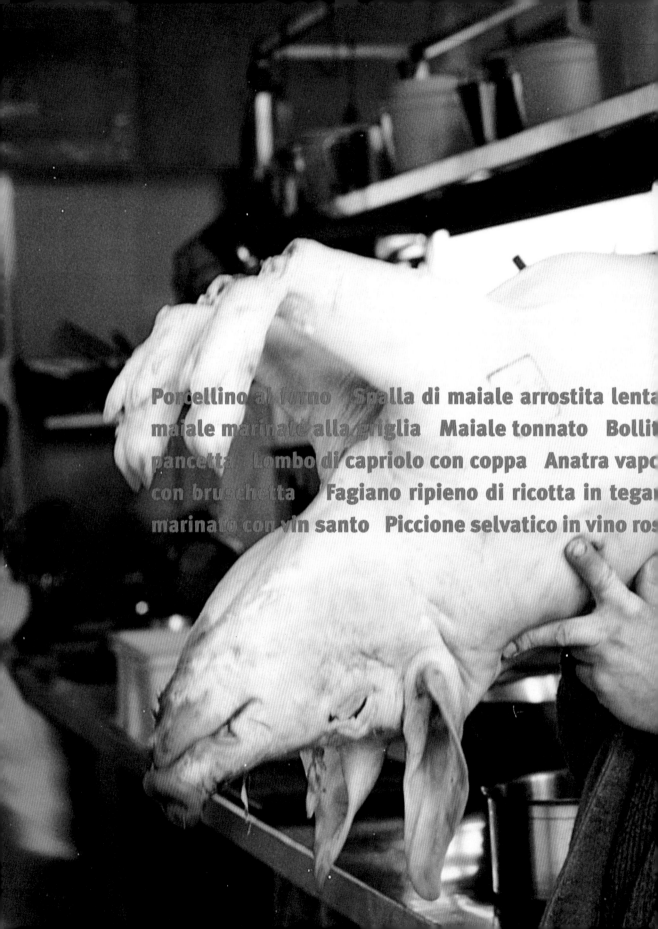

Porcellino al forno   Spalla di maiale arrostita lenta
maiale marinato alla griglia   Maiale tonnato   Bollit
pancetta   Lombo di capriolo con coppa   Anatra vapo
con bruschetta   Fagiano ripieno di ricotta in tega
marinato con vin santo   Piccione selvatico in vino ros

Lonza di maiale avvolta nella cotenna   Costate di
Faraona con latte e maggiorana   Pollo al sale con
rosto   Tetraone marinato nel latte   Tetraone ripiene
ernice con timo e mascarpone   Pi_one alla griglia

Porcellino al forno
Wood-roasted suckling pig

For 8 An eight-week-old pig weighs about 7.25 kg (16 lb). Pigs of 9 kg (20 lb) plus have more flavour, but they are too big for most domestic ovens. Order a pig that has had a cereal feed supplement for at least two weeks; this adds texture and taste.

1 suckling pig
6 garlic cloves, peeled
4 tablespoons fennel seeds
Maldon salt and coarsely ground black pepper
2 bunches fresh rosemary, leaves picked from the stalks
olive oil
300 ml (10 fl oz) Chicken Stock (see page 142) or water
1/2 bottle red wine

Preheat the oven to 230° C/450° F/Gas 8.

Crush the garlic in a mortar with the fennel seeds and 3 tablespoons salt. Add the rosemary leaves a little at a time, crushing together to make a rough paste. Add 2 tablespoons pepper.

Make fine scores in the skin of the pig wherever there is fat beneath the skin (very young pigs have practically no fat, so scoring is not possible). Rub the whole pig inside and out with the paste and into the scores. Brush with olive oil.

Place the pig on its side on a rack in a large roasting tray. You may have to curl it round to fit. Place in the hot oven and roast for 15 minutes, just to allow the skin to crackle, then carefully turn the pig on to its other side and roast for a further 15 minutes. The skin should be crisp on both sides.

Add the stock or water to the roasting pan. Turn the oven down to 160° C/325° F/Gas 3 and, basting from time to time, roast for 2.1/2-3 hours – longer if the pig is 9 kg (20 lb) and over. The pig is cooked when the shoulders and legs can be easily pulled away from the body.

Place the pig on a large preheated serving tray and set aside.

Remove as much fat as you can from the roasting tray. Place the roasting tray on the direct heat, add the red wine, and stir briskly to incorporate the meat juices. Season.

When carving the pig, place thick slices cut from the leg and shoulder and some rib chops on each plate along with a piece of crackling. Pour over each plate a little of the meat juices. Serve with wood-roasted vegetables (see pages 146-179) and Salsa Verde (see page 311).

Spalla di maiale arrostita lentamente
Slow-roasted shoulder of pork

For 8-10 Shoulder of pork is the most suitable cut of pork for this long method of cooking, as the meat is layered with fat which slowly melts away. We cook it overnight in the cooling wood oven.

1 small whole shoulder of pork, with skin, about 2.75-3.25 kg (6-7 lb) in weight
10 garlic cloves, peeled
100 g (4 oz) fennel seeds
Maldon salt and freshly ground black pepper
5-6 small dried red chillies, crumbled
juice of 5 lemons
3 tablespoons olive oil

Preheat the oven to 230° C/450° F/Gas 8. Using a small sharp knife, score the whole skin of the shoulder with deep cuts about 5 mm (1/4 in) wide.

Smash the garlic with the fennel seeds, then mix with salt, pepper and chilli to taste. Rub and push this mixture into and over the skin and all the surfaces of the meat. Place the shoulder on a rack in a roasting tin and roast for 30 minutes or until the skin begins to crackle up, blister and brown. Turn the shoulder and pour over half the lemon juice and 2 tablespoons of the oil. Turn the oven down, to 120° C/250° F/Gas 1/2, and leave the meat to roast, overnight or all day (from 8-24 hours). Turn over occasionally and baste with extra lemon juice and, if necessary, a little oil.

The shoulder is ready when it is completely soft under the crisp skin. You can tell by pushing with your finger: the meat will give way and might even fall off the bone. Serve each person with some of the crisp skin and meat cut from different parts of the shoulder. Add extra lemon juice to deglaze the pan, and spoon this over.

Lonza di maiale avvolta nella cotenna
Roast loin of pork wrapped in crackling

For 6-8 This loin of pork is a successful alternative to a whole suckling pig.

1/2 whole loin of pork with skin, rib end, about 2.75-3.25 kg (6-7 lb) in weight, boned
10 garlic cloves, peeled
4 tablespoons fennel seeds
Maldon salt and coarsely ground black pepper
juice of 2 lemons
3 tablespoons olive oil

Preheat the oven to 230° C/450° F/Gas 8.

Using a small sharp knife, score the skin of the loin with deep cuts about 5 mm (1/4 in) apart. Remove the scored skin from the loin, leaving only a thin layer of fat.

Smash the garlic in a pestle and mortar with the fennel seeds, then mix with 3 tablespoons sea salt and 1 tablespoon pepper. Rub and push this mixture into and over the skin and all the surfaces of the loin. Wrap the scored skin over the loin and tie on securely with string.

Place the loin on a rack in a roasting tray and put into the hot oven. Allow the skin to crackle up, blister and brown. Turn the loin and pour over half the lemon juice and 2 tablespoons of the oil. Turn the oven down to 200° C/400° F/Gas 6, and roast for 40 minutes. Every now and then turn over and baste with the juices. Turn the oven off and leave the loin in the oven with the door partially open for a further 25 minutes.

Serve each person with some of the crisp skin and meat cut from either end of the loin. Add a little lemon juice to deglaze the pan and spoon this over the meat.

Costate di maiale marinate alla griglia
Grilled marinated pork chops

For 6 Make sure the chops are cut from the centre loin which includes the fillet.

6 organic pork chops, about 2.5 cm (1 in) thick, fat removed
4 garlic cloves, peeled
3 tablespoons Maldon salt (less if using another salt)
2 tablespoons black peppercorns, coarsely ground
6 sprigs rosemary, leaves picked from the stalks, roughly chopped
juice of 3 lemons
6 tablespoons olive oil
6 lemon wedges

Place each chop on a piece of clingfilm at least 25 cm (10 in) square, and cover with a second piece of clingfilm. Using a wooden mallet, gently beat the chops to flatten them out until doubled in size. This takes time and patience. The beaten chops should be about 1 cm (1/2 in) thick. Place in a container large enough to hold them in one layer.

In a mortar, roughly pound the garlic with the salt, pepper and rosemary. Add the lemon juice and olive oil to liquefy the mixture. Spread this marinade over both sides of each chop, and leave in a cool place, covered, for about 1 hour.

Preheat the griddle pan or char-grill to very hot, and grill each chop for 5-6 minutes on each side. Serve with lemon.

Maiale tonnato
Pork tonnato

For 6 You can make this dish with leftover Roast Loin of Pork Wrapped in Crackling (see page 350), or cook the pork as below a day in advance.

about 2.25-2.75 kg (5-6 lb) rump end of loin of pork on the bone (or as above)
6 garlic cloves, peeled
1 bunch rosemary, leaves picked from the stalks
Maldon salt and freshly ground black pepper
juice of 1 lemon
1 x 250 g (9 oz) tin top-quality tuna in olive oil
1 recipe Anchovy-Caper Mayonnaise (see page 311)
12 salted anchovy fillets, prepared (see page 346)
100 g (4 oz) salted capers, prepared (see page 346)
3 tablespoons small basil leaves

Preheat the oven to 230° C/450° F/Gas 8.

Trim the fat from the top side of the pork, leaving about 1 cm (1/2 in) only. With a small sharp pointed knife, make small incisions along and around each rib bone. Using a pestle and mortar, crush the garlic, rosemary leaves and 2 tablespoons salt together to make a crude paste. Rub this paste into all the cuts and over the fat.

Place the loin on a roasting rack in a roasting tray and roast in the preheated hot oven. Turn the pork over after 20 minutes, and baste. Turn the oven down to 200° C/400° F/Gas 6, and continue to roast and baste for a further hour.

Remove the rack from the tray. Put the meat in the tray, pour over the lemon juice, baste for a final time, and return to the oven for a further 10-15 minutes. The meat should be cooked just beyond pink. Remove from the oven and allow to cool in the roasting tray – for at least 2 hours.

When the meat is completely cold, carefully cut the loin away from the bones. Try to keep it in one piece. Keep the solidified juices from the tray.

Trim any fat from the loin and carve the meat into very fine slices. Arrange these overlapping on a large serving plate. Spread the solidified meat juices over the slices. Season with salt and pepper.

Drain the tuna from its preserving oil, and mash it roughly with a fork. Add it to the mayonnaise, mix, and test for seasoning. Spread the mayonnaise over the pork slices, then arrange the anchovy fillets on top. Scatter with the capers, and place a few small basil leaves around.

Bollito misto
Boiled duck with chicken and cotechino

For 8-10 This alternative recipe for Bollito Misto requires careful timing, starting individual ingredients cooking at different times so that they 'finish' together. You need three large saucepans to hold the ducks, chickens and cotechino respectively.

3 small Gressingham ducks, about 1.3 kg (3.1/2 lb) each
2 large free-range chickens, about 2.75 (6 lb) each
3 precooked cotechino or 2 precooked zampone
Maldon salt and freshly ground black pepper
3 heads celery, hearts and leaves
12 organic carrots, scrubbed and halved lengthways
8 bay leaves
1 bunch fresh thyme
1 head garlic, quartered
1 bunch flat-leaf parsley
1 tablespoon white peppercorns
12 Roseval or Linska potatoes, peeled and halved lengthways, or 225 g (8 oz)
    cannellini beans or lentils, cooked (see page 346)

Fill a saucepan large enough to hold the ducks with enough water to keep the ducks completely submerged. Bring the water to the boil.

Remove the fat from the inside of the ducks, then season the cavities generously. Divide the leafy tops of the celery between the duck cavities, and place in each a halved whole carrot, 2 bay leaves, a sprig of thyme and a quarter of the garlic. Wrap each duck in a clean teatowel and then tie securely with string.

2 hours before serving Place the ducks into the boiling water and weight down to keep them submerged. Simmer for 2 hours. Remove, drain well and cool before unwrapping.

1 hour before serving After cooking the duck for 1 hour, put the chickens into another saucepan large enough to hold them. Add water to cover, as well as 2 celery sticks, 2 halved carrots, the remaining bay leaves and garlic, 3 sprigs of thyme, the parsley stalks and peppercorns. Bring to the boil, then simmer for about 1 hour.

30 minutes before serving Half an hour after you put the chickens on, place the zampone or cotechino in a separate saucepan and cook according to the instructions on the packet.

20 minutes before serving Add the remaining carrots, the celery hearts cut in quarters, and the potatoes if using to the simmering chickens and stock. Season the stock at this stage. Chop the parsley.

To serve Test the chickens for doneness by pulling a leg away from the body; it should come away easily if cooked. Remove from the pan and drain. Drain the vegetables, discarding the herbs and vegetables from the original stock. Strain and reserve the stock. Heat the cannellini beans or lentils if using.

Cut thick 1 cm (1/2 in) slices from the breast and leg of the ducks, the chickens into similar slices, using both white and brown meat, the cotechino or zampone into 1 cm (1/2 in) slices at an angle.

Arrange all the meats on a large warm serving plate and pour over some of the seasoned chicken stock. Arrange the carrots, celery and potatoes, cannellini beans or lentils around the meats, and scatter everything with parsley. Serve with Salsa di Dragoncello, Salsa di Rafano and mustard fruits (see pages 309, 304 and 347).

Faraona con latte e maggiorana
Guinea fowl pan-roasted with milk and marjoram

For 6

3 guinea fowl
1 bunch fresh marjoram
5 garlic cloves, peeled
Maldon salt and freshly ground black pepper
250 ml (8 fl oz) olive oil
250 ml (8 fl oz) vermouth
1 litre (1.3/4 pints) milk
peel of 2 lemons

Preheat the oven to 200° C/400° F/Gas 6.

Chop half the marjoram and 2 of the garlic cloves finely. Add the rest of the marjoram leaves, and season with salt and pepper. Add 1 tablespoon olive oil to hold it together.

With your hand gently separate the skin of the guinea fowl from the meat, and push a generous amount of herbs into the pocket between skin and meat of the breasts and legs. Put the rest of the garlic inside the birds. Place in a roasting tray.

Roast the guinea fowl in the preheated oven for 30 minutes, then add the vermouth to the dish, lower the heat to 170° C/340° F/Gas 3-4, and cook for 5 minutes. Add the milk and lemon peel, and cook for another 30 minutes.

Remove the guinea fowl from the oven and dish, and place on a heated plate. Put the roasting tin over a medium heat and bring to a gentle boil, scraping the juices. Let the liquid boil until you have a dark sauce. Pour over the guinea fowl and serve.

Pollo al sale con pancetta
Salt-roasted chicken wrapped in pancetta

For 6

3 small free-range organic chickens, about 1.1 kg (2.1/2 lb) each
Maldon salt and freshly ground black pepper
30 bay leaves, fresh if possible
3 lemons, washed, dried and pricked all over
500 g (18 oz) pancetta, thinly sliced
2 kg (4.1/2 lb) natural coarse sea salt

Preheat the oven to 180° C/350° F/Gas 4.

Wash each chicken well inside and out, and dry with kitchen paper. Season inside and out. Push half a handful of bay leaves into the cavities followed by a lemon. Push a few more bay leaves in with a slice of pancetta. Arrange the remaining pancetta, about 5 slices per bird, over the breasts, and tie to secure.

Place the chickens on their sides, side by side, in a large stainless-steel pan or casserole; they should fit snugly. Cover with the coarse salt, making sure that the salt packs down the sides, fills the spaces between each chicken and covers the breasts by at least 1 cm (1/2 in). Cover and put in the oven for 2 hours.

Test for doneness by breaking off a part of the salt crust and inserting the point of a knife into the leg – the juices should be clear and the meat moist but not pink.

Remove all the salt crust from the birds and brush off excess salt. Take the pancetta off the breast, cut the birds in half, and serve one-half per helping, with some of the pancetta and Salsa Verde (see page 311).

Lombo di capriolo con coppa
Loins of venison wrapped in coppa

For 8

1 saddle of roe deer, the 2 loins taken from the bone, and trimmed of fat and sinew

4 garlic cloves, peeled and thinly sliced

1 bunch fresh rosemary

50 g (2 oz) fat from prosciutto di Parma, or bacon fat, cut into slivers (as the garlic)

Maldon salt and freshly ground black pepper

500 g (18 oz) coppa di Parma, thinly sliced

50 g (2 oz) unsalted butter

2 tablespoons olive oil

300 ml (10 fl oz) red wine

Preheat the oven to 220° C/425° F/Gas 7. Place the loins on a board, and make small incisions along the grain of each, 5 cm (2 in) apart. Into each push a sliver of garlic, a sprig of rosemary, a small piece of prosciutto fat, and some salt and pepper. Both loins should be studded on all sides. Place two pieces of greaseproof paper on the board, and arrange the coppa slices over each, overlapping to form two rectangles that will accommodate the loins. Place the loins in the centre and roll up the papers so that each loin is completely wrapped in coppa. Remove the papers carefully. Tie the coppa wrapping in place with string.

Heat the butter and oil in a thick-bottomed roasting tray and seal the loins on all sides. Add half the red wine and roast for 20 minutes. Turn the loins over and roast for a further 15 minutes. Test for rare by pressing with your finger: it should feel soft and giving. For medium-rare, roast for a further 5 minutes. Remove to a serving platter. Deglaze the pan with the remainder of the red wine. Slice the meat thickly and serve with the pan juices.

Anatra vapore e arrosto
Steamed and roasted duck

For 6

2 Gressingham ducks, about 3 kg (3.1/2 lb) each
Maldon salt and freshly ground black pepper
8 garlic cloves, peeled
3 lemons, halved
4 celery stalks, with their leaves, roughly chopped
4 small carrots, scrubbed and roughly chopped
6 tablespoons balsamic vinegar
15 g (1/2 oz) unsalted butter

Preheat the oven to 200° C/400° F/Gas 6. Trim the neck skin from the ducks and remove all fat from the cavities. Using a fork, prick the duck skin in places where the fat deposits are thickest. Rub the whole ducks inside and out with sea salt.

Pulse-chop the garlic, 2 of the lemons, the celery stalks and leaves and the carrots. Add salt and pepper. Push this mixture inside each bird. Squeeze the remaining lemon over the birds, and set them breast side up in a roasting tray on a rack. Half fill the tray with boiling water. Completely cover the ducks with foil, wrapping it round the edge of the tray to make an airtight seal. Steam-bake for 1 hour. Remove the foil, and pour away the water. Pour half of the balsamic vinegar over the ducks and season the breasts. Turn the oven temperature up to 225° C/425° F/Gas 7. Roast for a further 15 minutes to brown the breasts, then turn the ducks over. Reduce the oven temperature to 200° C/400° F/Gas 6, and roast for a further 45-60 minutes. The skin should be dark brown and crisp, the flesh coming away from the bones.

Rest for 5 minutes before carving. Deglaze the roasting tray with the butter, balsamic and 1 tablespoon of lemon juice. Pour over each serving of duck and stuffing.

Tetraone marinato nel latte
Roast grouse marinated in milk

For 6

6 grouse
1 litre (1.3/4 pints) milk
Maldon salt and freshly ground black pepper
6 garlic cloves, peeled and crushed with the flat of a knife
1 bunch fresh sage, leaves picked from the stalks
1 bunch fresh rosemary, leaves picked from the stalks
350 g (12 oz) pancetta, thinly sliced
100 g (4 oz) unsalted butter
zest of 3 lemons
120 ml (4 fl oz) Vin Santo or other sweet wine

Place the milk in a container large enough to hold the birds, add salt and pepper and the garlic. Chop half the sage and rosemary and rub over each bird before placing them in the marinade. Leave for 1-2 hours in a cool place. Preheat the oven to 200° C/400° F/Gas 6.

Remove the grouse from the marinade and dry them. Wrap the breast of each bird in the pancetta slices, tying them on with string, and tucking sage leaves between the slices. Put some of the rosemary and a piece of garlic into each cavity. Melt the butter in two thick-bottomed casseroles, and brown three birds in each on all sides. Add enough of the marinade so that it comes about 1.5 cm (3/4 in) up the sides of the birds. Add the lemon zest, cover, place the birds in the preheated oven, and pot-roast, turning after 10 minutes, for a total of 20-25 minutes.

Place the birds on a serving platter. Reduce the casserole juices and add the Vin Santo. Check the seasoning and pour over the birds.

Tetraone ripiene con bruschetta
Roast grouse stuffed with bruschetta

For 6

6 grouse
6 slices sourdough bread (see page 277)
2 garlic cloves, peeled
1 large bunch fresh thyme
Maldon salt and freshly ground black pepper
extra virgin olive oil
350 g (12 oz) pancetta, thinly sliced
150 ml (5 fl oz) Chianti Classico

Preheat the oven to 230° C/450° F/Gas 8.

Ask the game dealer to leave the livers in the birds. Toast the sourdough bread on both sides, and rub whilst still warm with the garlic and some of the thyme. Season and drizzle each slice with extra virgin olive oil. Break the slices up into smallish pieces and stuff into the grouse. Place a sprig of thyme inside each bird as well.

Wrap each bird in the pancetta slices, tying them on with string. Heat a roasting tray, then brush lightly with oil. Brown the birds on all sides in the pan, then place in the preheated oven and roast for 20 minutes, a little longer if the birds are larger. Remove from the oven, place on a serving platter, and allow to rest for 5-10 minutes.

Deglaze the roasting pan with the Chianti. Pour this juice over each bird, pulling the bruschetta out from the cavity. Drizzle some extra virgin olive oil over, and serve with rocket or mustard leaves.

Fagiano ripieno di ricotta in tegame
Pot-roasted pheasant stuffed with ricotta

For 6

3 small hen pheasants
Maldon salt and freshly ground black pepper
500 g (18 oz) ricotta cheese
1 bunch fresh sage leaves
250 g (9 oz) pancetta, very thinly sliced
120 g (4.1/2 oz) unsalted butter
120 ml (4 fl oz) Vecchio Romagna or other dark brandy

Season the cavity of each bird and then fill with the ricotta and a few sage leaves. Lay the thin slices of pancetta over the breasts of each bird, inserting a sage leaf or two as well. Tie round each pheasant with string to secure the pancetta.

Use a thick heavy saucepan or casserole with a lid that the birds will fit into snugly. Put the butter in the pan and melt over a high heat. Brown the pheasants on all sides, then sprinkle with salt and pepper. Add any remaining sage leaves, cover with the lid, and turn the heat to low. Cook for about 45 minutes, turning the birds quite frequently and basting each time.

Remove the pheasants from the saucepan, and keep warm on a serving plate. Add the Vecchio Romagna to the pan and heat quickly, stirring to deglaze.

Remove the string and divide each pheasant into two. Serve with the cooked ricotta and the juices poured over.

Pernice con timo e mascarpone
Roast partridge with thyme and mascarpone

For 6

6 partridges, plucked and cleaned

Maldon salt and freshly ground black pepper

250 g (9 oz) mascarpone cheese

2 tablespoons each of fresh flat-leaf parsley, fresh marjoram and

fresh thyme, leaves picked from the stalks and chopped

350 g (12 oz) pancetta, thinly sliced

3 tablespoons olive oil

150 ml (5 fl oz) red wine or stock

Preheat the oven to 220° C/425° F/Gas 7.

Season the cavities of the partridges with salt and pepper.

In a bowl gently combine the mascarpone with the herbs, then season with salt and pepper. Place a large tablespoon of this mixture inside each partridge. Wrap the pancetta around the partridges and tie on with string.

Heat the olive oil in a roasting tray and brown the birds on all sides. Put in the preheated oven and roast for 15 minutes. Remove from the oven and place the birds on a warm plate while you make the sauce.

Pour out any fat from the pan, then deglaze with the red wine or stock. Add the remaining mascarpone and cook over a high heat for a minute. Pour over the partridges and serve.

Piccione alla griglia marinato con vin santo
Grilled bresse pigeon marinated in vin santo

For 6

6 Bresse pigeons
Maldon salt and coarsely ground black pepper
2 small dried red chillies, crumbled
1/2 head celery, leaves chopped, stalks finely sliced
1 small red onion, peeled and finely chopped
6 garlic cloves, peeled and sliced
1 bunch fresh thyme, leaves picked from the stalks
500 ml (17 fl oz) Vin Santo
3 tablespoons olive oil

To flatten the birds, using a large knife, make a cut down either side of the backbone and remove. Now use a small knife and carefully cut the body carcass and breast bones away from the meat. Spread each bird out flat, and place in a large flat dish. Season with salt, pepper and chilli, and scatter over the celery, onion, garlic and thyme. Add the Vin Santo and olive oil. Cover and marinate for 2-3 hours or overnight in the fridge.

Preheat the char-grill or griddle pan to medium hot. Remove the birds from the marinade; strain and keep the liquid. Place the birds on the grill, skin side down, and cook for 3-4 minutes, positioning the legs of each bird, which take longer to cook, on the hottest part of the grill. The breast should remain slightly pink. Turn and cook for a further 5-10 minutes. Spoon a little of the marinade over each bird in the final few minutes. Remove from the grill, and spoon a little more marinade over each bird whilst they rest.

Piccione selvatico in vino rosso
Wood pigeons braised in red wine

For 6

6 wood pigeons

2 tablespoons olive oil

1 red onion, peeled and roughly chopped

200 g (7 oz) pancetta, cut into matchsticks

5 garlic cloves, peeled and coarsely sliced

1 dried red chilli, crumbled

50 g (2 oz) dried porcini, soaked for 30 minutes in hot water, drained and roughly
    chopped

1 tablespoon cumin seeds

120 ml (4 fl oz) red wine

1/2 x 450 g (1 lb) tin peeled plum tomatoes, drained of their juices

8 juniper berries

Maldon salt and freshly ground black pepper

2 tablespoons Dijon mustard

Preheat the oven to 220° C/425° F/Gas 7. Use a heavy casserole with a lid. Heat the oil and seal the pigeons on all sides. Remove.

Fry the onion and pancetta in the hot oil and when soft, add the garlic, chilli and mushrooms. After 3 minutes add the cumin, then stir and cook for 5 minutes. Add the wine, tomatoes and juniper, and bring to the boil. Add the pigeons, breast side down. The liquid should come halfway up each bird. Cover and bake for 2 hours. Stir the mustard into the juices, season and serve hot or cold.

Bread
Brusc

Pizza

netta

10

Sourdough bread Pagnotta Pizza Pizza con cipo
e acciughe Pizza con robiola, tartufo bianco e tru
taleggio e tartufo bianco Bruschetta Crostini B
Bruschetta con cavolo nero e olio Bruschetta co
Bruschetta con acciughe marinate nel vino Crostini

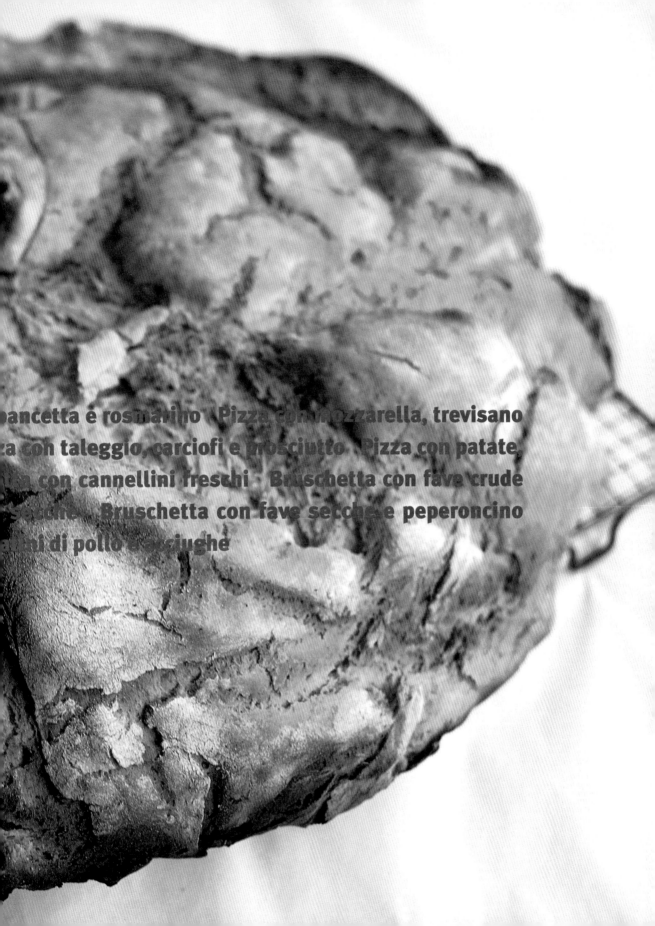

pancetta e rosmarino · Pizza con mozzarella, trevisano
za con taleggio, carciofi e prosciutto · Pizza con patate,
con cannellini freschi · Bruschetta con fave crude
ecche · Bruschetta con fave secche e peperoncino
ni di pollo e acciughe

Potato sourdough starter

Makes about 400 g (14 oz)

2 medium potatoes, peeled and cut into 2 cm (3/4 in) dice
water
plain bread flour

Cook the potatoes in 475 ml (16 fl oz) water until soft. Mash lightly with a fork into the water and leave to cool. Add 250 g (8 oz) of the flour and mix very thoroughly until you have a smooth batter. Put into a sterile glass jar or jug and seal tightly with clingfilm. Leave in a warm dark place for two days. (An airing cupboard is good.)

Stir the starter which will have begun to ferment and expand. Re-cover and leave for another day.

Uncover the starter, add 100g (4 oz) flour and 4 tablespoons warm water. Stir to mix. Cover again and put back in the warm place for two more days.

Uncover the starter and put into a warm bowl. Add a further 200 g (7 oz) flour and 4 tablespoons warm water. Mix together until the flour is incorporated, and then leave covered with a cloth to double in volume. It takes about 6 hours before the sourdough is ready for use. Store in the fridge, tightly covered with clingfilm.

Sourdough bread

Makes 2 loaves Use this bread for bruschetta.

400 g (14 oz) Potato Sourdough Starter (see previous recipe and page 347)
1.25 kg (2.3/4 lb) plain unbleached flour
600-720 ml (20-24 fl oz) warm water
2 tablespoons Maldon salt
4 tablespoons olive oil

Use a processor or mixer fitted with a dough hook.

Mix together the starter with the flour and half the water for about 8 minutes on slow speed. Remove, cover and leave in a warm place for 30 minutes. (If you wish to keep a sourdough going, remove 250 g/8 oz of this dough, and put into a clean bowl, cover with clingfilm and refrigerate.) Add the remaining water, the salt and olive oil, and stir together to combine. Return to the machine, and knead for a further 5 minutes – you should have a wet dough. Remove, place in a lightly oiled bowl, cover and leave to double in volume in a warm place, about 2.1/2 hours.

Place the dough on a floured surface and divide into two. Knead each piece roughly into two round loaves, and leave to prove for a further 2 hours.

Preheat the oven to 230° C/450° F/Gas 8.

Place the loaves on a floured baking tray, and make a cut across each. Place in the preheated oven after spraying the inside of the oven with water, using a spray bottle. Bake for 10 minutes, then check for browning. Turn if necessary. Spray the oven again, and reduce the heat to 200° C/400° F/Gas 6. Continue baking for a further 20-30 minutes. Turn the loaves over after 20 minutes. The bread is cooked when it sounds hollow after tapping. Cool on wire racks.

Pagnotta

Makes 1 large loaf Pagnotta is a semolina sourdough bread made in Puglia. Use it for bruschetta.

Stage 1

250 g (8 oz) Potato Sourdough Starter (see page 276)

1.2 litres (2 pints) warm water (at 27° C/80° F)

1 kg (2.1/4 lb) semolina bread flour, very finely ground

Stage 2

500 ml (17 fl oz) warm water (at 27° C/80° F)

2.5 kg (5.1/2 lb) semolina bread flour, very finely ground

250 g (8 oz) wholemeal flour

100 g (4 oz) Maldon salt

Stage 1 Make the 'sponge' in a warm place. Warm a mixing bowl, pour in the water, add the sourdough starter and mix together, making sure they combine well. Add the flour, and stir for a few minutes to a smooth consistency. Cover with clingfilm and leave in a draught-free place (not the fridge) overnight.

Stage 2 To make the bread dough, mix the sponge with the water, and half the semolina flour. Stir together until you have a sticky mass. (If you wish to keep a sourdough going, remove 250 g/8 oz of this sticky dough, and put into a clean bowl, cover with clingfilm and refrigerate.) Add the remaining flours and the salt, and knead the dough for at least 10 minutes, dusting with extra flour if needed to reduce its stickiness. The dough should become smooth and elastic. Alternatively, put half of your mixture at a time into a processor or mixer fitted with a dough hook and process for 10 minutes. Repeat with the second half of the dough. Combine the two by hand.

Place the dough on a warm lightly oiled baking sheet large enough for the loaf to expand for 5-6 hours in a warm and draught-free (not hot) place. When the dough forms large cracks, it is ready for baking.

Preheat the oven to 230° C/450° F/Gas 8.

Bake in the preheated oven for 20 minutes, then reduce the oven temperature to 180° C/350° F/Gas 4. Continue baking for another 40 minutes, turning the loaf over after 20 minutes. The loaf is cooked when it sounds hollow on tapping. Cool on a wire rack.

Pizza dough

For 6, making 6 x 25 cm (10 in) pizzas We use the basic pizza dough recipe from Alice Waters' Chez Panisse restaurant in Berkeley, California.

Step 1

4 teaspoons granular dried yeast

125 ml (4 fl oz) warm water

150 g (5 oz) rye flour

Step 2

250 ml (8 fl oz) warm water

2 tablespoons milk

4 tablespoons olive oil

1 teaspoon Maldon salt

500 g (18 oz) plain flour

Warm a bowl large enough to take the total dough mixture.

Mix the yeast with the 125 ml (4 fl oz) warm water in the warm bowl. When 'melted', add the rye flour and stir well to combine. Leave in a warm place to form a sponge, at least 30 minutes.

When the mixture has formed a sponge, add the remaining ingredients. Put the mixture in a processor or mixer fitted with a dough hook, and knead for 10-15 minutes. The dough will be quite wet and sticky (this texture will make a crisper crust).

Place the dough in a bowl greased with extra olive oil, and drizzle a little over the top. Cover with a cloth and leave to rise in a warm place for about 2 hours. Knock the dough back, and knead a couple of times then return to the bowl and let it rise for a further 40 minutes.

Preheat the oven to 230° C/450° F/Gas 8, and have ready a large flat baking tray or a pizza stone.

When the dough is ready, divide into six golf-ball-sized pieces, and individually form into balls. Roll out each ball on a floured surface with quick light motions as thinly as possible. A golf ball of this dough should roll out to make a 25 cm (10 in) pizza base.

Pizza con trevisano, pancetta e rosmarino
Pizza with trevise, pancetta and rosemary

6 x 25 cm (10 in) pizza bases (see page 280)
3 heads trevise
extra virgin olive oil
3 buffalo mozzarella, thinly sliced
2 branches fresh rosemary, leaves picked from the stalks, finely chopped
Maldon salt and freshly ground black pepper
200 g (7 oz) pancetta affumicata, thinly sliced

Pull the leaves from the thick white stalks of the trevise, and shred them. Wash thoroughly, and drain well. Toss with 2 tablespoons olive oil. Place the trevise on the pizza bases, followed by the sliced mozzarella, and scatter with rosemary, salt and pepper. Place the slices of pancetta over the top, about four per pizza. Drizzle lightly with a little more olive oil and bake in the preheated oven until the cheese has melted, the pancetta is cooked and the crust is crisp, about 6-8 minutes.

Pizza con mozzarella, trevisano e acciughe
Pizza with mozzarella, trevise and anchovies

6 x 25 cm (10 in) pizza bases (see page 280)
18 salted anchovy fillets, prepared (see page 346)
coarsely ground black pepper
2 lemons
120 ml (4 fl oz) olive oil
2 branches fresh rosemary, leaves picked from the stalks, finely chopped
3 medium or 2 large heads trevise
3 buffalo mozzarella, thinly sliced

Place the anchovy fillets in a dish. Sprinkle them with a little black pepper, the zest and juice of one of the lemons, and half the olive oil. Sprinkle the chopped rosemary over the fillets, and leave to marinate for a few minutes.

Remove the flimsy torn outer leaves of the trevise heads, and peel the stalks. Cut each head in half lengthways, then in half again if they are medium, into eighths if large. Toss with the remaining oil and lemon juice.

Scatter the trevise over the pizza bases, and place the mozzarella slices on top. Arrange the marinated anchovy fillets over the mozzarella, then bake in the preheated oven for 6-8 minutes until the dough is cooked. The mozzarella should just be melted, and the pizza rim crisp.

Pizza con robiola, tartufo bianco e rucola
Pizza with robiola, white truffle and rocket

Robiola is an unpasteurised, unpressed, cows' milk cheese.

6 x 25 cm (10 in) pizza bases (see page 280)
2 x 120 g (4.1/2 oz) Robiola cheese, cut into pieces
Maldon salt and freshly ground black pepper
4 tablespoons extra virgin olive oil
250 g (9 oz) rocket leaves
juice of 1/2 lemon
120 ml (4 fl oz) white truffle oil

Scatter the pieces of Robiola over the pizzas, then season with salt and pepper. Drizzle half the extra virgin olive oil over the pizzas and bake in the preheated oven until the dough is cooked.

Meanwhile, dress the rocket leaves with the remaining extra virgin olive oil and the lemon juice.

Remove the pizzas from the oven. Drizzle the truffle oil over the melted Robiola and scatter with a few dressed rocket leaves.

Pizza con taleggio, carciofi e prosciutto
Pizza with taleggio, artichokes and prosciutto

6 x 25 cm (10 in) pizza bases (see page 280)

6 small artichokes, prepared (see page 172)

2 tablespoons extra virgin olive oil

Maldon salt and freshly ground black pepper

2 garlic cloves, peeled and finely chopped

1 bunch thyme, leaves picked from the stalks

350 g (12 oz) Taleggio cheese, roughly cut, rind removed

300 g (10 oz) prosciutto, thinly sliced

In a heavy-bottomed pan, heat the olive oil, add the artichoke hearts, and season with salt and pepper, garlic and thyme. Cook the hearts, turning them continuously so they don't burn, for about 10 minutes. Remove from the pan and cool.

Dot the pieces of Taleggio over the pizza bases. Scatter the slices of artichoke heart over the Taleggio, then season with salt and pepper. Bake in the preheated oven until the dough is cooked. When ready, serve with a slice of prosciutto laid over the top of the pizza.

Pizza con patate, taleggio e tartufo bianco
Pizza with potato, taleggio and white truffle

6 x 25 cm (10 in) pizza bases (see page 280)

450 g (1 lb) Linska or Roseval potatoes, scrubbed clean

300 g (10 oz) Taleggio cheese, cut into thin slices, rind removed

Maldon salt and freshly ground black pepper

150 ml (5 fl oz) olive oil

1 x 50 g (2 oz) white truffle, carefully brushed clean

Slice the potatoes on the finest setting of the mandoline; they should be transparent. Leave in a bowl of cold water to remove the starch, then drain and pat dry.

Place the Taleggio over the pizza bases, and cover with the slices of potato. Season with salt and pepper, drizzle with oil, and bake in the preheated oven until the dough is crisp, about 6-8 minutes. Shave the truffle abundantly over the pizzas.

Alternatively, you can scatter the cooked pizzas with 200 g (7 oz) Parmesan shavings and drizzle with 100 ml (3.1/2 fl oz) white truffle oil.

Bruschetta

For 6

6 slices pugliese or sourdough bread, cut 1 cm (1/2 in) thick
1 large garlic clove, peeled
extra virgin olive oil

Toast the bread on both sides then lightly rub with the garlic. Drizzle with extra virgin olive oil then serve with your chosen topping.

Crostini

For 6

6 slices ciabatta bread, cut at an angle, 1 cm (1/2 in) thick
1 large garlic clove, peeled
extra virgin olive oil

Toast the bread on both sides then lightly rub with the garlic. Drizzle with extra virgin olive oil and serve with your chosen topping.

Bruschetta con cannellini freschi
Tomato bruschetta with fresh cannellini

For 6 The season for fresh cannellini beans is short, from August to September.

6 slices pugliese bruschetta (see page 290)

3 large ripe sweet tomatoes, halved

3 teaspoons dried wild oregano

3 small dried red chillies, crumbled

100 ml (3.1/2 fl oz) extra virgin olive oil

Cannellini beans

1.3 kg (3 lb) fresh cannellini beans in their pods

3 large garlic cloves, peeled

1 bunch fresh sage

2 large ripe sweet tomatoes

Maldon salt and freshly ground black pepper

Pod the beans, then place in a thick-bottomed saucepan. Cover with water, and add the garlic, sage and tomatoes. Bring to the boil, then turn the heat down, and gently simmer for 30-60 minutes according to freshness. They must not become mushy. Drain, remove the sage, garlic and any bits of tomato skin and stalk. Season with salt, pepper and olive oil.

Squash one half tomato on to each bruschetta, then sprinkle with some of the oregano and chilli. Drizzle with olive oil, then add a ladleful of warm cannellini beans to cover half of each bruschetta. Serve immediately.

Bruschetta con fave crude
Bruschetta with mashed broad beans

For 6

1.3 kg (3 lb) young broad beans, podded weight
2 garlic cloves, peeled
4 tablespoons fresh mint leaves
4 tablespoons freshly grated Pecorino cheese
4 tablespoons olive oil
Maldon salt and freshly ground black pepper
juice of 1 lemon
6 slices sourdough bruschetta (see page 290)

Pound the broad beans in a pestle and mortar with the garlic and mint. When the mixture is thick in texture, remove and place in a bowl. Stir in the Pecorino and the olive oil. Season with salt and pepper and the lemon juice and serve on the bruschetta.

Bruschetta con cavolo nero e olio
Bruschetta with cavolo nero and oil

For 6

12 leaves cavolo nero, washed and hard stalks removed
1 litre (1.3/4 pints) Vegetable Stock (see page 143) or water
Maldon salt and freshly ground black pepper
6 slices pugliese bruschetta (see page 290)
extra virgin olive oil

Bring the stock or salted water to a boil. Add the cavolo, lower the heat and simmer for 10 minutes or until soft. Put 2 pieces on top of each bruschetta. Pour on some oil, and season.

Bruschetta con erbe secche
Bruschetta with dried herbs

For 6

1 tablespoon each of dried oregano, thyme and marjoram (or one or two herbs)
1 teaspoon fennel seeds
6 slices sourdough bruschetta (see page 290)
3 dried red chillies, crumbled
Maldon salt and freshly ground black pepper
extra virgin olive oil

Scatter the herbs and seeds lightly over each bruschetta, then cautiously add the chilli, salt and pepper. Drizzle over extra virgin olive oil, and serve immediately.

Bruschetta con fave secche e peperoncino
Bruschetta with dried broad beans and chilli

For 6

500 g (18 oz) dried broad beans without skins
1 celery stalk
2 bay leaves
2 garlic cloves, peeled
4 tablespoons extra virgin olive oil
4 small fresh hot red chillies
Maldon salt and freshly ground black pepper
6 slices pugliese bruschetta (see page 290)

Soak the beans in cold water overnight. When ready to cook, preheat the oven to 180° C/350° F/Gas 4.

Drain the beans and place in an earthenware pot with a lid. Cover with water to twice the depth of the beans, and add the celery, bay and garlic. Cover and bake for 2 hours or until the water has been absorbed. The beans should be so soft that you can smash them to a pulp with a wooden spoon.

In a small pan heat the olive oil, and fry the whole chillies for a minute to allow them to cook and turn from red to red-brown. Add the whole fried chillies to your mashed beans, smashing them into the purée to break them up. Season and serve on the bruschetta.

Bruschetta con acciughe marinate nel vino
Bruschetta with anchovies marinated in wine

For 6

18 salted anchovies, washed

100 ml (3.1/2 fl oz) Chardonnay wine

freshly ground black pepper

1 dried red chilli, crumbled

zest and juice of 2 lemons

150 ml (5 fl oz) extra virgin olive oil

3 tablespoons finely chopped parsley

a handful of bitter leaves, blanched in boiling water (see method)

3 lemons, quartered

6 thick slices sourdough bruschetta (see page 290)

Place the anchovies in a bowl and cover with wine. Leave to marinate for 2 hours or overnight. Fillet each anchovy, lay out on a flat dish, and season with black pepper, crushed dried chilli and lemon zest. Drizzle over the olive oil and a few drops of the lemon juice. Scatter generously with parsley.

Serve the anchovies with blanched bitter greens such as cicoria, cime di rapa, cavolo nero or Swiss chard, the bruschetta and lemon quarters.

Crostini di fegatini di pollo e acciughe
Crostini of chicken livers with anchovies

500 g (18 oz) chicken livers
1 tablespoon olive oil
250 ml (8 fl oz) dry vermouth
6 salted anchovy fillets, prepared (see page 346)
2 teaspoons salted capers, prepared (see page 346)
250 ml (8 fl oz) Chicken Stock (see page 142)
Maldon salt and freshly ground black pepper
30 g (1.1/4 oz) unsalted butter
6 crostini (see page 290)

Remove any sinew and skin from the chicken livers, then wash and dry.

Heat the oil in a saucepan. Add the livers and cook for several minutes until brown, adding the vermouth from time to time, and scraping the juices from the bottom of the pan. Remove from the pan on to a board and chop with a mezzaluna until coarse. Return to the pan.

Chop the anchovies and capers until of the same consistency as the livers, then add to the livers. Cook for 10 minutes, adding several tablespoons of stock from time to time, to achieve a creamy consistency. Add salt and pepper and stir in the butter with a fork.

Put the livers on top of each crostini and serve.

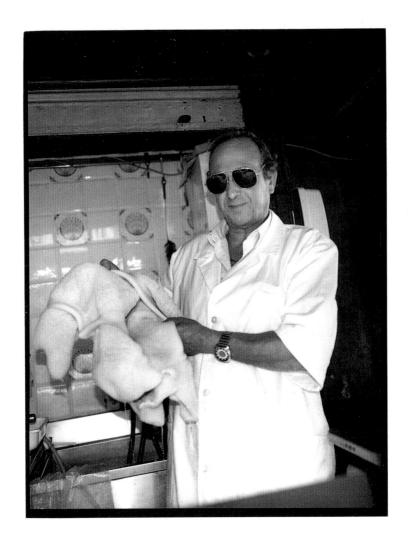

Sau

ces
11

Salsa di rafano Pomodoro concentrato Salsa di c
finocchio Salsa di aceto balsamico Salsa di bas
rosmarino Salsa calda d'acciughe Salsa di dragon
basilico Maionese con acciughe Salsa verde

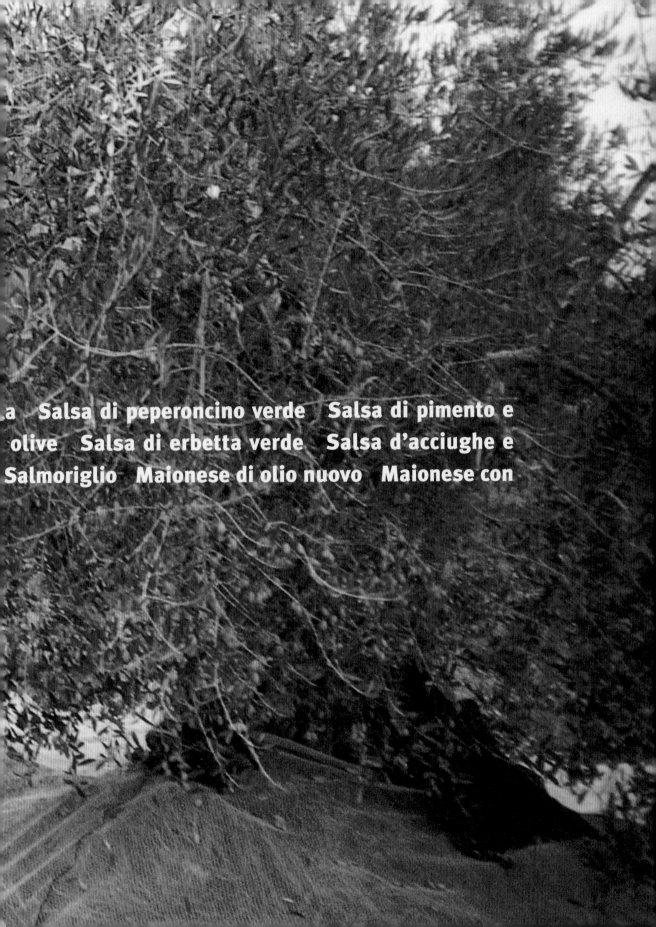

a   Salsa di peperoncino verde   Salsa di pimento e
olive   Salsa di erbetta verde   Salsa d'acciughe e
Salmoriglio   Maionese di olio nuovo   Maionese con

Salsa di rafano
Fresh horseradish

Serve with boiled meats.

200 g (7 oz) fresh horseradish, peeled
1 loaf ciabatta bread
4 tablespoons red wine vinegar
2 garlic cloves, peeled and finely chopped
150 ml (5 fl oz) olive oil
Maldon salt and freshly ground black
    pepper

Remove and discard the crust from the bread. Tear the bread into small pieces, then pulse-chop in the food processor to coarse breadcrumbs.

Place the breadcrumbs in a bowl, then add the vinegar and enough water to moisten the breadcrumbs. Put aside for 10 minutes before squeezing as dry as possible.

Grate the horseradish finely on the cheese grater. Combine with the garlic and squeezed breadcrumbs, then slowly add the olive oil, stirring continuously as for mayonnaise. Season with salt and pepper.

Pomodoro concentrato
Tomato and chilli paste

This is good with salt cod, or grilled aubergines.

1 x 800 g (1.3/4 lb) tin peeled plum
    tomatoes
1 tablespoon olive oil
2 garlic cloves, peeled and chopped
1 small red onion, peeled and finely
    chopped
3 red chillies, seeded and finely chopped
Maldon salt and freshly ground black
    pepper

In a heavy saucepan heat the oil and add the garlic, onion and chilli. Cook for 15 minutes over a low heat until very soft but not brown. Drain off some of the olive oil.

Return the pan to the heat, and add the drained tomatoes with a little juice. Cook over a low heat for 1.1/2 hours, when the sauce should be very thick and any remaining oil has risen to the top. Stir frequently throughout cooking to prevent the sauce from sticking.

Pour on to a flat plate and leave to cool. Serve in spoonfuls.

Salsa di cannella
Tomato and cinnamon

Serve with grilled lamb or grilled aubergine.

2 x 800 g (1.3/4 lb) tins plum tomatoes,
    drained of most of their juices
4 tablespoons olive oil
4 garlic cloves, peeled and thinly sliced
3 teaspoons coriander seeds, crushed
1-2 dried red chillies, crumbled
2 whole cinnamon sticks
Maldon salt and freshly ground black
    pepper

Heat the oil in a pan and gently fry the garlic, coriander seeds, chilli and cinnamon. When the garlic is golden brown, add the tomatoes and roughly break them up. Season with salt and pepper, and cook slowly, stirring occasionally, for at least 1.1/2 hours. Taste again for seasoning. The sauce should be thick and sweet with a hint of the chilli, coriander and cinnamon. Remove the cinnamon sticks before serving.

Salsa di peperoncino verde
Green chilli and lemon peel

This sauce is good with scallops, squid or grilled fish.

6 hot green chillies
1 lemon
Maldon salt and freshly ground black
    pepper
120 ml (4 fl oz) extra virgin olive oil

Seed and finely chop the chillies.

Cut the peel off the lemon (making sure there is no white pith), and slice into very fine strips. Combine with the chopped chilli. Add salt and pepper, and mix with the olive oil. Let sit for several hours before serving.

Salsa di pimento e finocchio
Fresh red chilli and fennel

Serve with grilled or roasted fish, or crab salad.

6 fresh chillies, seeded and finely chopped
50 g (2 oz) fresh green fennel herb or fennel
    bulb tops, chopped
1/2 garlic clove, peeled and finely chopped
    (optional)
Maldon salt and freshly ground black
    pepper
150 ml (5 fl oz) extra virgin olive oil
juice of 2 lemons

Combine the chilli, fennel, garlic if using, and seasoning. Cover with the olive oil and finally add the lemon juice.

Salsa di aceto balsamico
Balsamic red peppercorn

This is good with grilled fish or grilled lamb.

2 garlic cloves, peeled
3 tablespoons red peppercorns
Maldon salt and freshly ground black
    pepper
2 medium fresh red chillies, seeded and
    chopped
6 tablespoons balsamic vinegar
150 ml (5 fl oz) extra virgin olive oil
juice of 2 lemons
3 tablespoons chopped fresh flat-leaf
    parsley

Pound the garlic and peppercorns together in a pestle and mortar with a little salt.

When they are well crushed, add the chilli, balsamic vinegar, olive oil and lemon juice. Stir in the parsley, and season with salt and pepper.

Salsa di basilico e olive
Basil, olive and anchovy

We serve this sauce with grilled turbot or roasted turbot tranche (see page 230).

250 g (9 oz) small black Niçoise olives, stoned

6 salted anchovies, prepared (see page 346)

1 garlic clove, peeled and finely chopped

juice of 1 lemon

3 tablespoons balsamic or red wine (Volpaia 'Erbe') herb vinegar

150 ml (5 fl oz) extra virgin olive oil

4 tablespoons roughly chopped fresh basil leaves

Maldon salt and freshly ground black pepper

Roughly chop the olives and put in a bowl. Finely chop the anchovy fillets and add to the olives, along with the garlic. Stir in the lemon juice, vinegar and olive oil, then leave to marinate for 30 minutes before using.

Stir in the basil leaves and adjust the seasoning just before serving.

Salsa di erbetta verde
Green herb and pine nut

2 slices ciabatta bread, bottom crust removed

150 g (5 oz) pine nuts, lightly toasted

6 tablespoons fresh basil leaves, picked from the stalks, roughly chopped

3 tablespoons roughly chopped fresh flat-leaf parsley

3 tablespoons roughly chopped fresh mint leaves

50 g (2 oz) salted capers, prepared (see page 346)

2 tablespoons white wine vinegar

5 tablespoons extra virgin olive oil

1 teaspoon Maldon salt

freshly ground black pepper

Tear the ciabatta into pieces and roughly pulse-chop to coarse breadcrumbs.

Using a pestle and mortar, lightly pound the pine nuts, then stir in the herbs. Add the breadcrumbs and capers, and mix together with the vinegar and olive oil. Season with salt and pepper.

Salsa d'acciughe e rosmarino
Anchovy and rosemary

2 tablespoons finely chopped fresh
    rosemary
12 salted anchovy fillets, prepared (see
    page 346)
juice of 2 lemons
150 ml (5 fl oz) extra virgin olive oil

Crush the rosemary in a mortar, add the anchovies and pound to a paste. Slowly add the lemon juice, stirring to blend. Finally add the olive oil a drop at a time. When about half has been added, pour in the remainder in a thin, steady stream, stirring continuously. Alternatively, you can use a food processor although this method produces a thicker sauce. Put the rosemary in and chop very finely, then add the anchovy and chop to a thick, fine paste. Pour the oil in slowly. Finally, add the lemon juice.

Salsa calda d'acciughe
Warm anchovy

12 anchovies, salted preferably, prepared
    (see page 346)
3 garlic cloves, peeled
120 ml (4 fl oz) milk
4 tablespoons herb wine vinegar (Volpaia
    'Erbe')
freshly ground black pepper
150 ml (5 fl oz) olive oil

Gently simmer the garlic cloves in the milk until soft, about 15 minutes. Allow to cool.

Put the anchovies in a food processor and pulse-chop to a coarse texture. Add the soft garlic and a little of the milk, and pulse together to form a thick creamy consistency. Add the vinegar and black pepper.

Put this thick sauce into a small saucepan and gently heat. Slowly add the olive oil, stirring all the time. Serve hot.

Salsa di dragoncello
Tarragon

1/2 ciabatta loaf

65 ml (2.1/2 fl oz) red wine vinegar

the yolks of 2 hard-boiled eggs

100 g (4 oz) fresh tarragon, stalks removed,
  chopped

10 salted anchovy fillets, prepared (see
  page 346), chopped

50 g (2 oz) salted capers, prepared (see
  page 346), chopped

120-175 ml (4-6 fl oz) extra virgin olive oil

Tear the bread into small pieces, and soak in the vinegar for 20 minutes. Remove, squeeze dry, and chop, ideally with a mezzaluna.

Mash the egg yolks with a fork.

Very gently combine the bread, tarragon, anchovies, capers and egg in a bowl. Stir in the oil.

Salmoriglio
Summer thyme

Make in the summer, when lemon thyme has lush leaves, or use yellow thyme or large leaf thyme. Serve with vegetables, fish, chicken, carpaccio etc.

3 bunches fresh thyme, washed and
  spun dry

1 garlic clove, peeled

1 tablespoon Maldon salt

juice of 1.1/2 lemons

5 tablespoons extra virgin olive oil

freshly ground black pepper

Pick the thyme leaves from the stalks, and put them in a mortar with the garlic clove and salt. Crush until you get a fine green paste. Stir in the lemon juice to lubricate, then slowly add the olive oil. Test for seasoning, adding a little pepper. This has a strong salty taste to highlight the perfume of the thyme.

Maionese di olio nuovo
New olive oil mayonnaise

New olive oil has a special pungency in its first few months (November to the end of March).

2 medium egg yolks from very fresh organic
    eggs
500 ml (17 fl oz) new season extra virgin
    olive oil
juice of 1 fresh lemon
Maldon salt and coarsely ground black
    pepper

Use a pestle and mortar to make the mayonnaise.

Gently stir the yolks with the pestle and combine for a minute. Start adding the new oil drop by drop. Continue until the emulsion is very thick and sticky. At that point add a little lemon juice. Carry on adding oil and lemon juice until you have finished both and have a perfect thick, bright green mayonnaise. Season with salt and pepper.

Maionese con basilico
Basil mayonnaise

Extra virgin olive oil in the summer has lost its peppery quality and is ideal for making basil mayonnaise.

1 recipe New Olive Oil Mayonnaise, as left,
    using extra virgin olive oil
6 tablespoons basil leaves, stalks removed
2 garlic cloves, crushed with a little Maldon
    salt

Make the mayonnaise as left. Crush the basil leaves in a pestle and mortar with the garlic and salt to form a wet purée. Add to the mayonnaise at the end.

Maionese con acciughe
Anchovy-caper mayonnaise

2 medium egg yolks from very fresh organic
eggs
500 ml (17 fl oz) extra virgin olive oil
juice of 2 lemons
Maldon salt and coarsely ground black
pepper
10 salted anchovy fillets, prepared (see
page 346), roughly chopped
4 tablespoons salted capers, prepared (see
page 346), roughly chopped
2 tablespoons finely chopped fresh flat-leaf
parsley

Make the mayonnaise as in New Olive
Oil Mayonnaise left, using the juice of
one of the lemons only. Mix the juice of
the second lemon with the anchovies
and stir into the mayonnaise, then stir
in the capers and parsley.

Salsa verde
Green sauce

1 large bunch fresh flat-leaf parsley, leaves
picked from the stalks
1 bunch fresh basil, leaves picked from the
stalks
a handful of fresh mint leaves
3 garlic cloves, peeled
100 g (4 oz) salted capers, prepared (see
page 346)
6 salted anchovy fillets, prepared (see page
346)
2 tablespoons red wine vinegar
5 tablespoons extra virgin olive oil
1 tablespoon Dijon mustard
Maldon salt and freshly ground black
pepper

If using a food processor, pulse-chop
the parsley, basil, mint, garlic, capers
and anchovies until roughly blended.
Transfer to a large bowl and add the
vinegar. Slowly pour in the olive oil,
stirring constantly, and finally add the
mustard. Check for seasoning.

This sauce may also be prepared by
hand, on a board, preferably using a
mezzaluna.

Cream
Fruit Ice

ortes

Cream

12

Panna cotta con grappa e lamponi   Panna cotta a
cioccolato amaro e nocciole arrostite   Torta di mand
valpolicella   Bruschetta di albicocche, peschenoci e
Gelato alle prugne   Gelato al limone e ricotta   Gela
Granita al limone   Granita al caffè   Granita alla mela

llo   Crema di mascarpone   Monte bianco   Torta di
Torta di mandorle, limone e ricotta   Dolce estivo con
   Pere al forno con valpolicella   Gelato al ribes nero
vin santo   Gelato alla nocciola   Sorbetto alla pesci
   Tartufi di cioccolato amaro

Panna cotta con grappa e lamponi
Panna cotta with grappa and raspberries

For 6

1.2 litres (2 pints) double cream
2 vanilla pods
thinly pared rind of 2 lemons
3 gelatine leaves
150 ml (5 fl oz) cold milk
150 g (5 oz) icing sugar
120 ml (4 fl oz) grappa, plus extra to serve
3 punnets raspberries

Pour 900 ml (1.1/2 pints) of the cream into a pan, add the vanilla pods and lemon rind, bring to the boil, then simmer until reduced by one-third. Remove the cooked lemon rind and keep to one side. Remove the vanilla pods and scrape the softened insides into the cream.

Soak the gelatine in the milk for about 15 minutes or until soft. Remove the gelatine, heat the milk until boiling, then return the gelatine to the milk and stir until dissolved. Pour the milk and gelatine mixture into the hot cream through a sieve, stir, then leave to cool.

Lightly whip the remaining cream with the icing sugar, fold into the cooled cooked cream, then add the grappa. Place a piece of cooked lemon rind in each of six small 200 ml (7 fl oz) moulds or bowls, pour in the cream mixture and allow to set in the fridge for at least 2 hours.

Turn out on to dessert plates and serve with fresh raspberries and a tablespoon of grappa poured over the top.

Panna cotta a caramello
Panna cotta with caramel

For 6

1.2 litres (2 pints) double cream
2 vanilla pods
3 gelatine leaves
150 ml (5 fl oz) cold milk
150 g (5 oz) icing sugar
120 ml (4 fl oz) Vecchio Romagna (brandy), plus extra to serve
Caramel
250 g (9 oz) caster sugar
175 ml (6 fl oz) water
4-6 pieces thinly pared orange rind
1 x 5 cm (2 in) cinnamon stick
120 ml (4 fl oz) freshly squeezed orange juice

To make the caramel, place the sugar, water, orange rind and cinnamon in a heavy-bottomed saucepan. Slowly bring to the boil to melt the sugar, then boil to reduce to a thick dark caramel. Cool, remove the cinnamon, then stir in the orange juice. Wet six 200 ml (7 fl oz) bowls, then spoon 2 tablespoons of the caramel into each.

Make the basic Panna Cotta as in the previous recipe, substituting Vecchio Romana for the grappa. Pour into the dishes on top of the caramel, then allow to set in the fridge for at least 2 hours.

Turn out on to dessert plates, and serve with a little Vecchio Romagna over the top.

Crema di mascarpone
Mascarpone cream

For 6 At La Vecchia Osteria near Follonica, this is served as a dessert with cantuccini biscuits. It is also delicious with summer fruits and berries.

500 g (18 oz) mascarpone cheese
3 very fresh, free-range, organic egg yolks
120 g (4.1/2 oz) icing sugar

Beat the mascarpone lightly. In a separate bowl, beat the egg yolks. Add the icing sugar to the egg yolks, then fold into the mascarpone. Keep cool until you serve.

Monte bianco

For 6

500 g (18 oz) fresh chestnuts
1 litre (1.3/4 pints) milk
100 g (4 oz) caster sugar
2 vanilla pods, split open and seeds loosened
250 g (9 oz) crème fraîche
a little good-quality bitter chocolate

Bring a large saucepan of water to the boil.

Using a small sharp knife, score the fresh chestnuts across the round sides of their outer shells. Drop them into the boiling water and boil for 15-20 minutes according to size. Remove a few chestnuts at a time to shell them; the shell will come off easily so long as the chestnuts are kept hot in the cooking water. Squeeze each chestnut to crack the shell open, then prise the nuts out of the shell. Remove the bitter inner skin.

Heat the milk in a large pan, add the sugar, split vanilla pods and the shelled and skinned chestnuts, and simmer gently for 40 minutes until the chestnuts become quite soft; the liquid will have reduced.

Put the cooked chestnuts through a coarse mouli. Add enough of the remaining reduced milk to bring the mixture together to form a thick dough. Test for sweetness.

Using a small plain nozzle, pipe the chestnut dough out into a mountain shape on a flat serving platter; this will take some time! Serve with crème fraîche with some bitter chocolate grated on top.

Torta di cioccolato amaro e nocciole arrostite
Bitter chocolate roasted hazelnut torte

For 16

500 g (18 oz) shelled hazelnuts

500 g (18 oz) Callebaut chocolate, or other dark bitter-sweet chocolate with a
minimum of 68% cocoa butter

500 g (18 oz) unsalted butter, at room temperature

500 g (18 oz) caster sugar

12 medium organic eggs

Preheat the oven to 150° C/300° F/Gas 2. Line a 30 x 6 cm (12 x 2.1/2 in) cake tin with buttered greaseproof paper.

Roast the hazelnuts in the preheated oven until their skins become crisp and the nuts begin to colour, about 20 minutes. Place the hot nuts in a tea towel, fold over and rub on a flat surface in the towel. This removes most of the skins. Place the skinned nuts in a food processor and pulse-chop to a rough texture, not a fine flour. Set aside.

Break the chocolate into small pieces and place in a bowl over a saucepan of simmering water. Allow to melt. Do not stir. Using an electric mixer, beat the soft butter with the sugar until light and fluffy. Slowly add the liquid chocolate, allowing it to blend in. Add the eggs one by one, continuing to mix gently. When all the eggs are incorporated, remove the whisk and fold in the crushed nuts.

Pour the mixture into the prepared cake tin, and bake for 40-50 minutes. Test for doneness with a skewer – it should come out dry. Turn off the oven, but leave the torte in it, with the door slightly ajar, for a further 30 minutes. Remove from the tin when completely cool.

Torta di mandorle
Almond tart

For 10-12

350 g (12 oz) plain flour
a pinch of salt
225 g (8 oz) unsalted cold butter, cut into cubes
100 g (4 oz) icing sugar
3 organic egg yolks
Filling
350 g (12 oz) unsalted butter, softened
350 g (12 oz) caster sugar
350 g (12 oz) blanched whole almonds
4 organic eggs

For the sweet pastry, pulse the flour, salt and butter in a food processor until the mixture resembles coarse breadcrumbs. Add the sugar then the egg yolks and pulse. The mixture will immediately combine and leave the sides of the bowl. Remove, wrap in cling film, and chill for at least an hour.

Preheat the oven to 180° C/350° F/Gas 4. Coarsely grate the pastry into a 30 cm (12 in) loose-bottomed fluted flan tin, then press it evenly on to the sides and base. Bake blind for 20 minutes until very light brown. Cool. Reduce the temperature to 150° C/300° F/Gas 3.

For the filling, cream the butter and sugar until the mixture is pale and light. Put the almonds in a food processor and chop until fine. Add the butter and sugar and blend, then beat in the eggs one by one. Pour into the pastry case and bake for 40 minutes. Cool and cover with seasonal fruits.

Torta di mandorle, limone e ricotta
Almond, lemon and ricotta cake

Makes 1 x 25 cm (10 in) cake

250 g (9 oz) blanched almonds
65 g (2.1/2 oz) plain flour
finely grated zest of 7 lemons, juice of 3 lemons
225 g (8 oz) unsalted butter, softened
250 g (9 oz) caster sugar
6 organic eggs, separated
300 g (10 oz) fresh ricotta cheese

Preheat the oven to 150° C/300° F/Gas 2. Butter a 25 cm (10 in) round cake tin, and line with greaseproof paper.

Coarsely chop the almonds in a food processor. Combine with the flour and lemon zest. Beat the butter and sugar together in a mixer until pale and light. Add the egg yolks one by one, then add the almond mixture.

Put the ricotta in a bowl and lightly beat with a fork. Add the lemon juice. In another bowl, beat the egg whites until they form soft peaks. Fold the egg whites into the almond mixture and finally stir in the ricotta.

Spoon the mixture into the prepared tin and bake in the preheated oven for 35-40 minutes until set. Test by inserting a skewer, which should come out clean. Remove from the tin while still warm, and cool on a cake rack.

Dolce estivo con valpolicella
Summer pudding with valpolicella

For 8

1 sourdough loaf, crust removed and cut into 1 cm (1/2 in) slices (see page 277)
675 g (1.1/2 lb) blackcurrants (or small strawberries), stalks and leaves removed
675 g (1.1/2 lb) redcurrants, stalks and leaves removed
675 g (1.1/2 lb) raspberries (or blackberries)
300 g (10 oz) caster sugar
100 ml (3.1/2 fl oz) water
1 bottle Valpolicella Classico
3 vanilla pods, split lengthways
juice of 1 lemon

Wash the fruit and shake dry. Dissolve the sugar in the water in a thick-bottomed pan, then boil until the syrup begins to colour a light caramel. Remove from the heat, carefully add the Valpolicella and stir.

Add 450 g (1 lb) of each fruit plus the vanilla pods to the hot syrup, and return to the stove. Heat gently, stirring, until the fruits begin to release their juices. Try not to break the fruit up. Remove from the heat. Add the lemon juice and uncooked fruit.

Line a 25 cm (10 in) bowl with the bread, so that there are no gaps. Keep aside enough slices to cover the top. Pour the fruit mixture into the bowl; it should easily come to the top, the juices soaking into the bread. Cover with a layer of bread slices, pushing them into the fruit to soak up the juice. Weigh down with a small plate that just fits into the bowl. Put in the fridge for at least 4 hours.

Turn out and serve with a few fresh berries and crème fraîche.

Bruschetta di albicocche, peschenoci e susine
Apricot, nectarine and plum bruschetta

For 6

6 apricots
6 very ripe soft nectarines
6 plums
6 x 1.5 cm (1/2 in) slices from a sourdough loaf, bottom crust removed (see page 277)
100 g (4 oz) unsalted butter, softened
2 vanilla pods
250 g (9 oz) caster sugar
50 ml (2 fl oz) Vecchio Romagna (brandy)
crème fraîche to serve

Preheat the oven to 200° C/400° F/Gas 6.

Butter a baking tray. Butter each slice of bread on one side only.

Cut the vanilla pods into small pieces, and pound with the sugar in a mortar. Alternatively, roughly chop the vanilla with the sugar in a food processor.

Halve the fruits and remove the stones. Put the fruits together in a bowl. Stir in the vanilla sugar and the brandy. Leave to marinate for 20 minutes or so.

On each buttered slice of bread break and press two halves of nectarine, cut side down, so that the bread absorbs the juices. Place two halves of apricots and plums, cut side up, on top of each slice, and pour over the remaining juices from the bowl.

Bake the bruschettas in the preheated oven for 25 minutes. They should be crisp on the edges and the fruits cooked. Serve warm with crème fraîche.

Pere al forno con valpolicella
Baked pears with valpolicella

For 6

6 ripe Comice pears
zest (in slices) and juice of 1 lemon
3 tablespoons caster sugar
1 vanilla pod, split
200 ml (7 fl oz) Valpolicella (red wine)
2 tablespoons soft brown sugar
Caramel
50 ml (2 fl oz) balsamic vinegar
300 g (10 oz) caster sugar
120 ml (4 fl oz) water

Preheat the oven to 180° C/350° F/Gas 4.

Cut a thin slice off the bottom of the pears. Hollow out the core from the bottom. Put a slice of lemon zest, 1/2 tablespoon of sugar and some of the vanilla seeds inside each pear. Put the pears upright in a baking dish. Sprinkle with lemon juice, cover with foil, and bake for 10 minutes until the juice has been absorbed. Remove the foil.

To make the caramel, heat the sugar and water together gently to melt the sugar, then boil. Remove when very dark, and beginning to smell bitter. Carefully add the Valpolicella. Pour over the pears, and bake for 40 minutes longer, basting every 10 minutes until the pears are slightly shrivelled.

Remove from the oven and sprinkle with soft brown sugar and vinegar. Serve with crème fraîche.

Gelato al ribes nero
Blackcurrant ice cream

For 6

1 kg (2.1/4 lb) blackcurrants
300 g (10 oz) caster sugar
juice of 1 lemon
500 ml (17 fl oz) double cream

Remove the stalks and leaves from the blackcurrants, then wash and shake them dry.

Put them into a suitable large saucepan. Add the sugar and gently heat, stirring to break up the fruit. As soon as the juices begin to flow and the blackcurrants change colour to deep red, remove. Allow to cool and then push the fruit juice and pulp through a fruit sieve. Add the lemon juice.

In a separate bowl very lightly whip the cream only to slightly thicken. Fold 1 serving spoon of cream into the fruit purée, then quickly return this to the cream. Stir gently to combine. Put into an ice-cream machine and churn until frozen, or freeze in a suitable container.

Gelato alle prugne
Plum ice cream

For 10

2 kg (4.1/2 lb) small dark-skinned plums
15 organic egg yolks
500 g (18 oz) caster sugar
1.75 litres (3 pints) double cream
450 ml (15 fl oz) milk
2 vanilla pods, split

To make the custard, slowly beat the egg yolks and 350 g (12 oz) of the sugar together until pale and thick, about 10 minutes. Heat the cream and milk with the vanilla pods until just below boiling point.

Pour a little of the hot cream into the egg mixture to combine. Return to the saucepan and cook gently, stirring constantly, until the custard thickens. Do not allow it to boil. Pour out into a bowl and cool.

Wash the plums and put into a large saucepan with a good fitting lid. Add the remaining sugar, cover and gently heat to boiling point. Remove and allow to cool. Push the fruit and juices through a sieve or mouli.

Carefully stir the custard into the plum purée, a ladleful at a time. Test for strength and sweetness, and remember that ice cream should taste sweeter before freezing. According to the type of plum, you may not need to add all the vanilla custard. Judge by taste.

Pour the mixture into an ice-cream machine and churn until frozen, or freeze in a suitable container.

Gelato al limone e ricotta
Lemon and ricotta ice cream

For 10

1.75 litres (3 pints) double cream
450 ml (15 fl oz) milk
20 organic egg yolks
350 g (12 oz) caster sugar
500 g (18 oz) ricotta cheese
juice and zest of 7 lemons

Combine the cream and milk in a heavy saucepan, and heat until just below boiling point. Remove from the heat.

Whisk the egg yolks and sugar together until light and fluffy, about 10 minutes. Mix a little of the warm cream into the eggs, then transfer the whole lot, including the remaining cream, back to the saucepan. Heat over a very low flame, stirring constantly to prevent curdling. Remove when the mixture is thick, just below boiling point. Cool.

Roughly break up the ricotta, but not too much, otherwise the texture of the ice cream will be lost. Add the lemon zest and juice and the ricotta to the cream mixture, and mix briefly. Pour into an ice-cream machine and churn until frozen, or freeze in a suitable container.

Gelato con vin santo
Vin santo ice cream

For 10 Vin Santo is the Tuscan dessert wine made from grapes that are left to dry from October to January. They are then pressed to make a concentrated yield which is aged in special small oak casks called Caratelli for at least four to five years.

20 organic egg yolks
400 g (14 oz) caster sugar
1 litre (1.3/4 pints) double cream
3/4 bottle Vin Santo

In a mixer (or in a bowl, using an electric hand-mixer), beat the egg yolks and sugar together until they have trebled in volume and are light. Transfer to a large bowl over a pan of simmering water. The water must not touch the bowl. Cook this custard, stirring constantly, until the mixture thickens and coats the back of the wooden spoon. Just before boiling point, taste to check that the eggs are cooked, then leave to cool.

Slightly whip the double cream and stir into the cooled custard, along with the Vin Santo. Pour into an ice-cream machine and churn until frozen, or freeze in a suitable container.

Gelato alla nocciola
Hazelnut ice cream

For 10 The intensity of the flavour depends on the careful roasting of the hazelnuts.

600 ml (1 pint) double cream

1.75 litres (3 pints) milk

15 organic egg yolks

350 g (12 oz) caster sugar

Praline

500 g (18 oz) shelled hazelnuts with skin

450 g (1 lb) caster sugar

300 ml (10 fl oz) water

Preheat the oven to 200° C/400° F/Gas 6.

Combine the cream and milk in a large heavy saucepan and heat until just below boiling point. Remove from the heat.

Whisk the egg yolks and sugar together until light and fluffy, about 10 minutes. Mix a little of the warm cream into the egg yolks then transfer the whole lot, including the remaining cream, back to the saucepan. Cook over a very low flame, stirring constantly to prevent curdling. Remove when the mixture is thick and just below boiling point. Pour into a bowl and cool.

Put the hazelnuts in a tin in one layer, and then into the preheated oven for 5 minutes. Remove, peel off the skins, then return to the tray, now lightly oiled. Put back in the oven and bake until browned but not burnt.

To make the caramel for the praline, dissolve the sugar and water in a saucepan and boil until almost smoking. Pour over the hazelnuts in the tin and let cool until solid.

Break up the praline and blend in a food processor to as fine as possible. Add to the ice cream mixture and stir well.

Pour the ice cream mixture through a fine chinois sieve. Put the bits of praline left in the chinois in a saucepan and cook until dark brown, about 5-6 minutes. Return to the chinois and press through, then stir into the ice cream.

Put the mixture into an ice-cream machine and churn until frozen, or freeze in a suitable container.

Peach sorbet

For 6

10 peaches
300 g (10 oz) caster sugar
120 ml (4 fl oz) lemon juice

Blanch the peaches in just enough water to cover. Remove the peaches from the liquid and reserve both. Skin the peaches, then cut into quarters, removing the stones.

Reduce the peach blanching water until you are left with 200 ml (7 fl oz). Add the sugar and boil to a syrup.

Put the peaches in a food processor and blend to a coarse purée. Mix with the syrup and lemon juice.

Pour into an ice-cream machine and churn until frozen, or freeze in a suitable container.

Lemon granita

For 6

500 ml (17 fl oz) water
100 g (4 oz) caster sugar
250 ml (8 fl oz) lemon juice
finely grated zest of 1 lemon

In a heavy-bottomed saucepan bring the water and sugar to the boil, and cook until reduced by almost half. Remove from the heat and, when cool, add the lemon juice and lemon zest.

Pour into shallow ice trays or cake tins, and put in the freezer. Allow the liquid to partially freeze, about 20-30 minutes. Mash this with a fork to break up the ice crystals, then return to the freezer and leave for a further 20 minutes. Repeat this process, mashing up the frozen liquid, then returning to the freezer and freezing, until you have a hard, dry, crystalline granita. This takes about 2.1/2 hours. As granita melts quickly, serve immediately.

Coffee granita

For 6

1 litre (1.3/4 pints) espresso coffee made in
     an espresso machine (use about 250 g/
     9 oz coffee)
300 g (10 oz) caster sugar

Make your espresso by your preferred
method. Whilst hot, dissolve the sugar
in it. Allow to cool. Test for sweetness
and strength, and add a little water if
too strong.

Place the liquid into shallow ice trays or
cake tins and put into the freezer. Allow
the coffee to partially freeze, about 20-
25 minutes. Mash this with a fork to
break up the ice crystals, then return to
the freezer and leave for a further 20
minutes. Repeat this process, mashing
up the frozen coffee, returning to the
freezer and freezing, until you have a
hard, dry, crystalline granita. Use
immediately. Serve with crème fraîche.

Pomegranate granita

For 6

15 ripe pomegranates, to make 1 litre
     (1.3/4 pints) pomegranate juice
3 lemons
300 g (10 oz) caster sugar
100 ml (3.1/2 fl oz) bitter Campari

Cut the pomegranates in half and
squeeze as for oranges. Strain out the
seeds and pith. Squeeze the lemons in
the same way. Stir the sugar into the
lemon juice, then add the pomegranate
juice. Taste for sweetness. Add the
Campari and stir well to make sure the
sugar has completely dissolved.

Pour the liquid into shallow ice trays or
cake tins, and put in the freezer. Allow
the juice to partially freeze, about 20-
30 minutes. Mash this with a fork to
break up the ice crystals, then return to
the freezer and leave for a further 20
minutes. Repeat this process, mashing
up the frozen juice, returning to the
freezer and freezing, until you have a
hard dry crystalline granita. This takes
up to 2.1/2 hours. Serve with crème
fraîche.

Tartufi di cioccolato amaro
Bitter chocolate truffles

Makes 450 g (1 lb)

150 ml (5 fl oz) double cream
400 g (14 oz) bitter chocolate, broken into small pieces
4 tablespoons unsalted butter, softened
best quality unsweetened cocoa powder

In a saucepan boil the double cream until it reduces to 2 tablespoons. Remove from the heat and stir in the chocolate until melted. Add the butter and stir gently, then pour into a large flat plate. Put into the fridge for approximately 45 minutes until chilled and set.

With a teaspoon scrape across the chocolate so that it forms a rough truffle shape, in large curls, not round balls! Roll them in the dry cocoa powder. Put them in the fridge for at least half an hour before serving.

Notes on ingredients

This is not intended to be a comprehensive glossary, but to provide information on certain specific ingredients which we use in our cooking. For more information on ingredients, see the glossary in *The River Cafe Cook Book*.

Anchovies The best salted anchovies come from Spain, from the fishing ports of Omdarroa and Zumai on the Bay of Biscay. The season lasts from April to June. The fish are caught, sold, graded, salted and packed all on the same day. First the anchovies are graded by size, the largest and most perfect being called 'Bar 1'. These are always packed in 10 kg tins. 16 kg of fresh anchovies are carefully layered with coarse sea salt in and on top of the tins, using a collar, then pressed with cement blocks over a period of three months until they fit into the tin. Anchovies graded 'bar 2' are salted and packed in the same way in 10 kg and 5 kg tins. Anchovies graded 'bar 3' and 'bar 4' are the smaller fish. They are selected, salted and packed into large barrels and pressed in the same way for three months, then washed, filleted and preserved in olive oil. Spanish salted anchovies from 10 kg tins are sold all over Italy, usually by the gram. Stalls selling just salted fish can be found in many markets. Ortiz, the finest brand, can be found in specialist shops in the UK. We buy 'Ortiz Bar 1' anchovies for the restaurant whenever possible.
To prepare salted anchovies taken dry from the tin, rinse under a slow-running cold tap to wash off any salt and carefully pull each fillet off the bone. Pat dry and use immediately or cover with extra virgin olive oil.

Borlotti and Cannellini Beans **To prepare** dried borlotti and cannellini beans, first soak overnight in a bowl of cold water to which you have added 2 tablespoons of bicarbonate of soda. **To cook** (for 250 g /9 oz dried beans), first drain the beans, rinse well and put in a saucepan with 1 large fresh tomato, a handful of fresh sage and 1/2 bulb of garlic, unpeeled. Cover with cold water, bring to the boil, then reduce the heat and simmer gently for 1-1.1/2 hours. Remove any froth or scum that comes to the surface. When the beans are tender, remove the tomato, sage and garlic but keep the beans in the cooking water until ready to use.

Brandy Vecchio Romagna 'Etichetta Nera' is a rich-flavoured Italian brandy made from a blend of wine spirits from Trebbiano di Romagna grapes. It is matured in small oak casks and aged for three years.

Capers Capers are the small flower buds of a shrub that grows wild throughout the Mediterranean. The smallest capers, considered the best, come from the island of Pantelleria. After picking, the buds are dried in the sun then salted.
To prepare salted capers, rinse thoroughly under a running cold tap for 1 minute. Taste to check if they are still salty. Leave to soak in a bowl of cold water for half an hour. Rinse again and use immediately or cover with red wine vinegar.

Chickpeas To skin drained chickpeas after cooking, lay them out on a clean tea towel, cover and rub with a circular motion to loosen the skins. Place the rubbed chickpeas in a bowl of cold water – the loose skins should rise to the top. Skim off the skins, drain the chickpeas and use.

Eggs Organic eggs with a dated laying stamp are the best to use, especially for ice cream. They also carry a stamp showing that they are approved by an organic certifying body. If eggs are not date-stamped, test by breaking an egg open on to a flat plate. The yolk should remain ovoid and the white should be thick, jelly-like and hold its shape. We buy eggs from Martin Pitt (see page 351).

Farro This is a type of hard wheat known as 'spelt' in English. It has been grown and used in Italy since Roman times and is now mostly grown in Lazio, Umbria and Abruzzo. A famous wedding soup of these regions is called 'Confarrotio'.

Honey Raw honey is from bees which have not been fed sugar and which has not been heat-treated or filtered during extraction.

Lentils Castellucio lentils are grown only in Norcia, an arid plain specifically designated by the Italian government as a lentil-growing area. The totally organic production by a farmers' co-operative is obliged to conform to very high standards. Castellucio lentils are available from specialist shops (see page 351).

To cook lentils, put them in a small saucepan, cover with cold water, bring to the boil, then skim. Add 1 clove of garlic and a celery stalk, turn the heat down, and simmer gently for 35 minutes or until the lentils are cooked. Drain and season. Remove and discard the garlic and celery.

Mustard fruits Mostarda di cremona is a piquant preserve traditionally served with Bollito Misto. It is made of candied fruits such as peaches, apricots, pears, figs and cherries, which are preserved in a honey, white wine and mustard syrup.

Olive oil The kind of extra virgin olive oil we use for cooking is different to the estate-bottled oils we use for pouring over bruschetta and adding to soups. The cooking oil is a blend of several extra virgin olive oils from all over Italy, produced from olives that are pressed when they are fully ripe and have dropped from the trees. Ripe olives produce more oil when pressed and have a higher acidity. The resulting oil has little flavour or aroma but is much cheaper and is fine for general cooking.

Estate-bottled cold-pressed extra virgin olive oils have very distinctive characteristics and flavours. We go to Italy every November to coincide with the olive harvest and choose oils to use in the restaurant in the coming year. Tuscan oils, which are thick, green and fruity, have always been our favourite. We choose two that complement each other from different estates and our current extra virgin olive oils are from Selvapiana and Felsina.

The oil from the Selvapiana estate is pressed from the 'Frantoio' variety. The olive trees grow alongside the famous vineyards in the cooler Chianti Ruffina zone north-east of Florence. The olives are picked early, when green, and pressed in a modern cold press, producing the greenest and most intensely spicy oil.

The new oil is bottled immediately and arrives in the restaurant by December, where our customers enjoy Bruschetta al'olio nuovo – a joy that excites us all.

At the Felsina estate in Castelnuovo Baradenga, on the southernmost borders of Chianti Classico, the olives are pressed in the old traditional way. The estate's mill at Farnetella has been run by the same man for the last 45 years. A manual process results in 15 litres of oil from 100 kg of olives. The olives are the 'Corriegiolo' variety, the greenest of all olives. They are hand-picked and crushed the same day, producing an incredibly fresh, green smooth oil that we have chosen for its long life, low acidity and subtle pepperiness. We use this oil for salads and blanched vegetables throughout the year.

Salt Maldon sea salt is pure flaky crystals free from all additives, a completely natural product with a better flavour than table salt and rich in natural minerals. Because of its intense flavour, you use less.

Natural coarse sea salt comes mostly from Spain and France. The grains are slightly smaller than young peas and contain desirable trace elements and minerals. The salt is unrefined and is sometimes grey in colour. Use this for salting fish, chicken and pasta water.

Sourdough starter The starter is the essential element in a sourdough loaf. Sourdough is basically flour and water which have fermented at 27° C (80° F) over 6-10 days, developing the wild yeasts and organisms present in the flour. A sourdough loaf has a distinctive open texture and a strong, slightly tangy taste. It keeps well and is more digestible than many other breads.

As it takes time and patience to develop a starter, we suggest you ask any baker who makes sourdough to sell you a piece of theirs (see also page 351).

Vinegar The estate of Castello di Volpaia at Radda, in Chianti, makes wonderful wine vinegars - 'Erbe', with herbs, 'Orto', with vegetables, and 'Spezie', with spice. We use all three flavours in salads and wood-roasted vegetables. They are available from specialist shops (see page 351).

Index

Suppliers

London

General ingredients

I Camisa and Sons
61 Old Compton Street
W1V 5DN
tel: 0171 437 7610

The Fifth Floor Food Market
Harvey Nichols
SW1X 7RJ
tel: 0171 235 5000

Fratelli Camisa Ltd
53 Charlotte Street
W1P 1LA
tel: 0171 255 1240

Gazzano & Son
167 Farringdon Road
EC1R 3AL
tel: 0171 837 1586

Joy
511 Finchley Road
NW3 7BB
tel: 0171 435 7711

La Fromagerie
30 Highbury Park
N5 2AA
tel: 0171 359 7440

Lina Stores
18 Brewer Street
W1R 3FS
tel: 0171 437 6482

Luigi's
349 Fulham Road
SW10 9TW
tel: 0171 352 7739

Mortimer and Bennett
33 Turnham Green Terrace
W4 1RG
tel: 0181 995 4145

The Real Food Store
14 Clifton Road
W9 1SS
tel: 0171 266 1162

Selfridges Food Hall
400 Oxford Street
W1A 1AB
tel: 0171 629 1234

Villandry
89 Marylebone High Street
W1M 3DE
tel: 0171 224 3799

Organic meat, game, fish

Blagdens Fishmongers
65-66 Paddington Street
W1M 3RR
tel: 0171 935 8321

Condon Fishmongers
363 Wandsworth Road
SW8 2JJ
tel: 0171 622 2934

Lidgate Butchers
110 Holland Park Avenue
W11 4UA
tel: 0171 727 8243

Planet Organic
42 Westbourne Grove
W2 5SH
tel: 0171 221 7171

Randalls Butchers
113 Wandsworth Bridge Road
SW6 2TE
tel: 0171 736 3426

Sourdough bread and sourdough

Baker and Spice
46 Walton Street
SW3 1RB
tel: 0171 589 4734

Clarke's
122 Kensington Church Street
W8 4BH
tel: 0171 229 2190

De Gustibus
53 Blandford Street
W1H 3AF
tel: 0171 486 6608

Planet Organic (see above)

Outside London

General ingredients

The Fine Cheese Company
29 Walcot Street
Bath BA1 5BN
tel: 01225 483407

Felix van den Berghe
40 High Street
Westbury on Trym
Bristol BS9 3DZ
tel: 0117 975 4240

The Cambridge Cheese Company
All Saints Passage
Cambridge CB2 3LS
tel: 01223 328672

Food for Thought
191 Ashley Road
Hale
Altrincham
Cheshire WA15 9SQ
tel: 0161 928 8052

Fratelli Sarti
133 Wellington Street
Glasgow G2 2XD
tel: 0141 248 2228

Cooks Food Hall
15 Castle Market Street
Dublin 2

Valvona and Crolla Ltd
19 Elm Row
Edinburgh EH7 4AA
tel: 0131 556 6066

Organic eggs

Martin Pitt
Levetts Farm
Clench Common
Marlborough
Wilts SN8 4DS
tel: 01672 512035

Organic meat, poultry, eggs

The Old Dairy Farm Shop
Path Hill Farm
Whitchurch on Thames
Berks RG8 7RE
tel: 0118 984 2392

Organic vegetables

Sunnyfields Organic Farm
Jacobs Gutter Lane
Totton
Southampton SO40 9FX
tel: 01703 871408

Sourdough bread and sourdough

Innes
Highfields
Clifton Lane
Statfold
Tamworth
B79 0AQ
tel: 01827 830097

Books

Food Lovers' Guide to Britain,
Henrietta Green, BBC Books

The authors would like to thank: Chefs **Lucy Boyd,** Theo Randall, **Darren Simpson,** Samantha Clark, Celia Harvey, **Christine Osmond,** Jamie Oliver, Alison Manning, **Garry Wilson** Editors Denise Bates, **Susan Fleming** Design **David Eldridge** Photographers Jean Pigozzi, **Martyn Thompson** Extra photographers Ossie Gray, Tom Kime, **Kenneth Gray,** Michael Elkin Touch-ups Jon Summerill Field trips **David Gleave All staff past and present at the River Cafe,** David MacIlwaine, Richard Rogers

First published in 1997   1 3 5 7 9 10 8 6 4 2   Text copyright © Rose Gray and Ruth Rogers 1997 Illustrations copyright © Martyn Thompson and Jean Pigozzi 1997   All rights reserved. No part of this publication may be reproduced, stored in a retrieval system, or transmitted in any form or by any means, electronic, mechanical, photocopying, recording or otherwise, without the prior permission of the copyright owners.   Rose Gray and Ruth Rogers have asserted their right to be identified as the authors of this work.   First published in the United Kingdom in 1997 by Ebury Press, Random House, 20 Vauxhall Bridge Road, London SW1V 2SA   Random House Australia (Pty) Limited, 20 Alfred Street, Milsons Point, Sydney, New South Wales 2061, Australia   Random House New Zealand Limited, 18 Poland Road, Glenfield, Auckland 10, New Zealand   Random House South Africa (Pty) Limited, Endulini, 5a Jubilee Road, Parktown 2193, South Africa   Random House UK Limited Reg. No. 954009   Paperback edition first published in 1998. A catalogue record for this book is available from the British Library.   ISBN 0 09 185170 X (hardback) ISBN 0 09 186419 4 (paperback)   Printed and bound in Great Britain by Butler and Tanner Limited